TEACHING AND LEARNING IN THE AGE OF COVID19

FAITH-BASED—ONLINE *AND* EMERGENCY REMOTE

EDITED BY

SEBASTIAN MAHFOOD, OP, PH.D.

TIMOTHY WESTBROOK, PH.D.

VICTORIA DUNNAM, PH.D.

En Route Books and Media, LLC
St. Louis, MO

⊕ *ENROUTE*
Make the time

En Route Books and Media, LLC
5705 Rhodes Avenue
St. Louis, MO 63109

Cover credit: Dr. Sebastian Mahfood, OP

Copyright © 2021 Sebastian Mahfood, Timothy Westbrook, and Victoria Dunnam

Library of Congress Control Number: 2021930932
ISBN-13: 978-1-952464-49-2 and 978-1-952464-65-2

CONTENTS

Engaging the Learner

FOREWORD

In early 2020, many of us began to confront an impending storm of challenges to previously-held notions of how we deliver education. Some of the first signs began happening in residentially-based classes and the sudden shift to emergency remote teaching (which some equated with online education). For others, the need to expand infrastructure to accommodate increased digital or online capacities became a far greater priority. In all of this, both students and faculty had to adjust expectations and approaches in a short amount of time. This opened doors for greater collegiality and collaboration as we continued exploring ways to accommodate rapidly changing educational norms.

My favorite movie, *Life is Beautiful*, tells the story of Jewish-Italian Guido who marries Dora. Guido and Dora have a son and live happily together until the occupation of Italy by Nazi forces. As fate would have it, they're deported to a concentration camp, and in an attempt to hold his family together and help his son survive the horrors of a concentration camp, Guido reconfigures detainment as a game with the goal of winning the grand prize, a tank. He shifts and re-shapes the paradigm of horror and reality to one that allows his son to see it as a chance to win the game. That movie is a reminder of the need to shift an existing paradigm to one that may be forged by uncertainty and yet an opportunity to help shape a renewed educational standard. I think now, more than ever, we have the occasion to shape and influence the conversation surrounding education no matter the context. This book outlines a pathway forward to doing just that. The dissonance we've experienced is part of creating a new or different paradigm.

It seems that three themes have emerged from this educational tectonic plate shifting. Those areas are collaboration, cohesiveness, and clarification. This shift has allowed us an opportunity to leverage social networks in a way that draws upon the creative, imaginative, and intelligent work that characterizes much of what our colleagues have done. This book highlights that work and the collaboration of leaders in online theological education. The term that is dominating our world right now is social distancing, but it would seem that rather than distance, we've been able to leverage our social networks as a way to influence broader contexts. We are collaborating with one another, and, in some ways, it allows us to redefine how we shape learning and teaching.

Online education has long taken the brunt of comparisons between online and residential. The dichotomy between the two usually results in an either/or paradigm rather than what best serves the student. As we shift the conversation from *what is the best platform* to *what is in the best interest of the student,* we may begin to see an educational paradigm that is much different from how we currently operate. For one, I believe it positions us to deliver a stronger product. The reality is that we don't operate in isolation from other elements in our educational ecology. The learning theories that we employ are taken from philosophies that form both platforms of learning. Our educational system has to begin looking toward a future that more seamlessly blurs the lines and situates itself within a larger ecosystem of learners, learning platforms (that include the residential classroom), and learning itself.

The shift to cohesion can lessen the impact of the dissonance we've experienced. I sometimes think about the conversations we had after Hurricane Katrina and the devastating impact on institutions of higher education in that area. The movement from largely residentially-based education to one that reflected online capabilities took some time. Similarly, we were ill-prepared for the seeming sudden shift the pandemic brought to education because of, in small part, the silos we've built. A successfully integrated system creates a stronger one so that when one silo goes down, it doesn't have to take the entire system with it. A diverse ecosystem is one that continues to thrive and flourish even when one of the trees or plants or shrubs falter or fail. A cohesive and integrated system builds in for calamity by looking at redundancy measures which allows it to shift in a more agile manner. If we can begin to shift the paradigm from *have-to* to *want-to* and see the inherent benefits of an integrated system, we position ourselves for a much stronger future.

In all of this, we're having to clarify our identity. It requires that we sharpen our focus on who (or whose) we are and what we are about. This is, at its core, a missional issue. It might be more helpful to situate ourselves within the larger mission and purpose of theological education and how we might be co-missioners in the pursuit of teaching and learning in a way that advances Kingdom work. Do our institutions, and our roles in them, fit with who we think we are and what we think we're doing? Are we posturing ourselves in a way that expands our borders beyond our institutional identity? Clarifying vision means that we're going to have to do some extended assessment to figure out if we're ready to embrace some re-shaping of our identity.

In all of this, I see more opportunities than challenges surrounding theological education. We've been given a chance to shape environments where the glass is not just half full but overflowing. This book intends to do just that; it's a continuation of a long-needed conversation. I trust its readers will feel welcomed to join us in that conversation.

- Mary E. Lowe, Ed.D.
  Online Associate Dean
  John W. Rawlings School of Divinity at Liberty University

INTRODUCTION

Sebastian Mahfood, OP

The chapters in this book focus on the kind of experimentation and innovation that has occurred in the development of distributed learning environments within theological education over the first two decades of the 21st century. It is specifically repackaged as a response to the coronavirus pandemic with which this third decade of the third millennium was launched.

The point is clear—we have it within ourselves already to address the current needs of our seminaries and theological schools that have found themselves thrust over the past year into a world of *emergency remote teaching and learning* with an increased, even federally-sponsored engagement in distributed learning methods such as online education.

Many of us have been in this field long enough—even longer for some—to remember the assistance provided by the Lilly Foundation through the Wabash Center in its 1999 and 2000 grant distribution to 72 theological schools of $300,000 each for the purpose of retrofitting our buildings to accommodate the use of appropriate technologies in our oncampus teaching and learning environments.

We whose careers were established by these grants remember spooling thousands of feet of cable, designing the initial internet and email networks, building the smart classrooms, developing server rooms and computer labs, setting up learning management systems like Moodle and Blackboard, and training faculty and students through their initial resistance into the normative use of these tools in the advancement of our schools' mission statements.

We reached the point by the end of the decade that the establishment of a Technology in Theological Education Group (TTEG) within the Association of Theological Schools seemed reasonable and necessary. Charles Willard, director of assessment and institutional evaluation at ATS, formed such a group in the spring of 2008, which was then organized and chaired by Sebastian Mahfood, who worked alongside an advisory board for the next half decade.

By 2013, enough positions with titles like "Director of Distance Learning" or "Online Learning Director" had been established among the theological schools that it made sense for a new group to emerge from within TTEG that ultimately called itself the Faith-based Online Learning Directors (FOLD), which now includes members from about five dozen theological schools. It's a portion of that membership that has produced this book, which is composed of twelve chapters that lay out processes by which to engage the literature and the learner on the use of distributed learning technologies in the Age of COVID-19.

The book begins with Dave Bland's chapter, entitled "Online Homiletical Pedagogy as Difficult Conversation," which was first presented at the Academy of Homiletics meeting in Louisville, Kentucky, during the annual meeting in December of 2013. The theme for the paper presentations that year was "Preaching As Difficult

Conversation." Understandably opposition to teaching performance classes online is strong. The author begins with observation, describing the phenomenon of the online environment and context. He then assesses its strengths and weaknesses based upon his role as a participant observer and on the critique of other written resources. He finally offers brief suggestions for strengthening his own online course as well as ideas others might consider as they reflect on the online format. This structure provides him with an organized way of studying his online experience as he engages in self-assessment.

Rebecca Hoey and Fawn McCracken's chapter entitled "Compensation and Ownership: The Current State of Online Course Development at Christian Colleges" discusses concerns regarding fair compensation and ownership rights that have historically been barriers to faculty participation in online course development while research from the past five years suggests colleges have evolved to develop policies and practices to address those concerns. Nonprofit private Christian colleges have less history offering online programs than their public and for-profit counterparts, and therefore their policies and culture may be less developed. Member institutions of the Council of Christian Colleges & Universities (CCCU) were surveyed to determine the current state of online course compensation and ownership practices at nonprofit private Christian colleges, and to examine potential relationships between compensation, ownership, and number of online programs. Findings from participating institutions suggest that the vast majority of CCCU member institutions compensate faculty for their work in course development, and those institutions have policies in place that give ownership jointly or exclusively to the institution. While the mean range for compensation of $1000-$2500 was similar to the mean range reported for course development in the literature, the total range suggests CCCU institutions have a top compensation rate lower than the top rate of public, for-profit, and other nonprofit institutions. There was no relationship between ownership of online courses and the number of online programs at CCCU institutions, which may mean other factors including compensation had more influence on faculty participation in the development of online programs. Future research should examine the efficacy of different compensation structures with respect to faculty participation in and satisfaction with online course development, and the commonalities and ramifications of specific arrangements for shared ownership of online courses.

Kelly Price, Julia Price, and Deborah Hayes' chapter entitled "Online Doctoral Students at a Faith-Based University: Concerns of Online Education" discusses how online doctoral education enrollment continues to rise while the number of academic institutions who offer the degree are increasing proportionately. Various types of institutions are involved in this growth, including those that are faith-based. Due to the competitive nature of all online doctoral degrees, including faith-based and secular programs, it is imperative to understand the needs and concerns of the students who enroll in such programs. Students enrolled in a faith-based university online doctoral program were surveyed regarding their concerns about online doctoral education. The results revealed three main themes of concerns/non-concerns, and these results could be beneficial to faith-based institutions who offer online doctoral education or plan to do so in the future.

Timothy Paul Westbrook, Morgan McGaughy, and Jordan

McDonald's chapter entitled "An Investigation into the Implications of Dewey's 'Learning Situation' For Online Education" discusses how course designers and program administrators face daily challenges of finding balance between new technology and educational principles conducive to online learning environments. This study investigates the implications of Dewey's understanding of the "learning situation" through a phenomenological inquiry into the experiences of students' participating in an online course at a faith-based liberal arts university. The salient themes of *flexibility, travel,* and *communication* emerged from the study. Ecology of learning and community of inquiry are treated in order to explore theoretical bridges between Dewey and distance education. A conceptual diagram of Dewey's learning situation is provided to assist online course designers in creating assignments that account for various levels of self-directed student reflection and online social interaction. The article concludes by recommending practical ways to infuse student experiences as part of student learning outcomes.

Victoria Dunnam's chapter entitled "Teaching Presence (Course Design, Direct Instruction, and Facilitated Discourse) and the Impact on Student Success in Online Learning" discusses how Online learning is becoming more prominent today because of COVID-19 and how our institutions have collectively embarked on offering emergency remote teaching in education. Exploring areas of online activities and how to move from teaching face-to-face into the online environment can be daunting for many seasoned educators. Questions on how to move from face-to-face to online teaching are unchartered areas for many in education. Questions on how to post documents online for students to read, how to use Zoom to hold class in the same way as in face-to-face class times, and how to add quizzes or discussions to the online environment pose many challenges during this critical time. Many articles have been written to help educators learn the importance of student collaboration and student engagement within online assignments. This chapter gives some insight on Victoria's experience as an Instructional Designer and Content Developer in online learning. She also shares a portion of her own research that examined student interactions in online courses in order to provide information about "teaching presence" in online learning.

Sunday Akin Olukoju's chapter entitled "Engaging Online Students Through Customer Service and Pastoral Care Mentality" reviews current reality and offers some ideas on how to engage online students creatively. Gleaning from over a decade of online teaching experience and given the spiritual formation piece that seminary education mandates, this chapter introduces customer service and pastoral care mentality in generating a learning environment that not only enriches and empowers online students, but also strikes a balance between rigor and vigor. In an age when the attention span is so short, this chapter also introduces some fun ideas that keep the classroom atmosphere warm, despite the physical and social distance between the various online students on one hand and the online students and their instructor on the other hand. This chapter acknowledges the importance of hard skills in midwifing a successfully efficient and effective online education delivery method and identifies some highly important soft skills that are indispensable to the entire business of online classroom delivery for it to be produced in the manner the designers intended.

Lawrence Hopperton's chapter entitled "Steps toward Equitable

Access for Faculty New to Online Learning" discusses the issue of disability compliance, which has long been thought to apply only to those courses that were designed and developed to be fully online, as it impacts traditionally oncampus faculty who have found themselves because of COVID-19 forced into *emergency remote teaching and learning* and are discovering the fuller range of their responsibility when engaging in distributed learning environments.

Matthew Boutilier's chapter entitled "Actively Engaging the Remote Learner" problematizes the online classroom's lack of physical presence in order to offer some tried and proven methods for engaging learners whose only connection to one another and to their course professor is through mediated means of communication.

Lawrence Hopperton's chapter entitled "Facilitating Learner-Centered Online Education" discusses how online learning incorporates the philosophy and methodology of experiential education, promoting inquiring forms of learning that engage learners in the experiences through which knowledge, both individual and collective, is created. Learning becomes an active and engaged, student-centered process driven by the situation with the online instructor serving as the expert course guide. This chapter presents ideas and best practices for teaching in the online environment. It summarizes accepted best practices for teaching in the post-secondary classroom and adapts these same practices to teaching in collaborative online learning. It shares specific tactics that can be used to enable engaged, collaborative, and student-centered learning.

Timothy Paul Westbrook's chapter entitled "eQuity: Considering 'Otherness' in the Online Classroom" discusses how we create learning spaces that give equitable opportunities for learning, especially when we have a diverse population of learners. Faith-based institutions that pursue fairness and equity and that provide moral guidance to students will not only survive, but will also help their students along the way to a greater understanding of the value the 'Other' adds to their own lives.

Lawrence Hopperton's chapter entitled "Flipped Classrooms: Reshaping the Tyndale Degree Completion Program for Engagement and Learning" presents a brief overview and general model of the flipped classroom with specific reference to Tyndale University's Degree Completion Program (DCP). He introduces the DCP as a five-week alternative learning approach for the completion of the last few credits for a degree, a process that has been subject to considerable criticism. Comments such as "You cannot deliver a full undergraduate course within the five-week requirement" are common and raise concerns about the validity and consistency of the learning outcomes. The flipped classroom, however, provides us with a fluid model for adapting content delivery and augmenting the utility of the components of education. Given the history of the DCP program, Hopperton asks whether it can create a flipped-classroom format that affords students greater autonomy and also helps the faculty deal with individuals and full classes while maintaining and augmenting academic outcomes.

Sebastian Mahfood and Michael Hoonhout's chapter entitled "Building an Online Course for the Catholic Distance Learning Network: Teaching Theology and Science in Cyberspace" was first published in *Seminary Journal* in 2008 and discusses the practical considerations that went into the redevelopment of a face-to-face course into an online course as part of a larger initiative to form a network of Catholic seminaries that could field online courses available at no cost to all seminarians in the country on the basis of their reciprocal agreements.

Naturally, more remains to be said than what is contained in these twelve chapters, and the editors of this book, Sebastian Mahfood, OP, Timothy Westbrook, and Victoria Dunnam, hope that we have provided a contextual frame within which that ongoing conversation may occur. We are especially grateful to the contributing authors, whose biographies are listed at the end of the book, and to the Association of Theological Schools that has been such a support to all of our schools over the past two decades of technology integration.

Engaging the Literature

1

Online Homiletical Pedagogy as Difficult Conversation[1]

Dave Bland

Engaging the Difficult Conversation of Online Education

Steve Delamarter (2005b) interviewed faculty from forty-five different theological seminaries across North America identifying twenty-six concerns they expressed about online education under three different categories. The reservations expressed ranged all the way from practical concerns related to the cost of technology, to theological concerns like the inability to engage in mentoring online, to pedagogical concerns such as certain disciplines not lending themselves to an online learning environment. Delamarter found intense disagreement over whether or not preaching classes can be or even should be taught online. He shares the following tension that marks this conversation: "One dean told me of the 'fantastic' preaching course they were offering online; another dean said, ' . . . you would

---

[1] From "Online Homiletical Pedagogy as Difficult Conversation," by D. Bland, 2015, NET: An e-Journal of Faith-Based Distance Learning. Reprinted with permission. See distancelearningdirectors.org.

never, never, never, ever get preaching online'" (Delamarter, 2005, 136). Clearly entering into the world of online education, particularly as it relates to the discipline of homiletics, raises passionate feelings and creates difficult conversations. It is the pedagogical elephant in the room. What I propose to do in this paper is to describe and assess my experience with teaching preaching online. I do not offer what I do as an exemplary model of online education but as a starting point for engaging in the difficult conversation of participating in such an enterprise.

The first time I offered a preaching course online occurred during the fall of 2012. I found myself in a similar situation Richard Ward (2010) describes when he offered an online preaching course a few years ago. The administration had told me prior to 2012 that I needed to plan on teaching a preaching class online in the next couple of years. I had taught online classes before but not preaching classes. This was a new challenge, and it was difficult for me to understand how one could effectively offer a performance class online. Even though I am not technologically savvy and was not initially motivated, once I started learning and spending time with one or two individuals who were more technologically experienced, my enthusiasm slowly increased. These individuals were Angela Sivia and Carl Walker at Harding University who took major blocks of one-on-one time to teach me about the course delivery systems of Moodle and Canvas and the screencast software Camtasia and allowed me to interrupt them with numerous questions along the way. They all demonstrated an amazing amount of patience with me.

Between 2000 and 2013, our enrollment at Harding School of Theology (HST) in Memphis had steadily declined, as is the case with many seminaries across North America. There are a number of reasons why but two important ones rise to the toOne is the rising cost of seminary education. Our registrar calculated the average cost of the indebtedness of our 2013 graduates stood at $52,000. More and more students understandably are unwilling to accrue that kind of educational debt. The other major obstacle for declining enrollment is the inaccessibility of seminary education. The demographics of our students often make it difficult for them to be on campus. The average age of our students is thirty-three years old.[2] Ninety-one percent are married with two children and average working outside of class 32.5 hours a week (1986, p.160). Most students are already in a ministry context, many working in small rural congregations. Finances are tight. It is extremely difficult for them to uproot their families and move to Memphis. It is important to find a way to provide educational opportunities to this constituency. Whereas the online class may not result in a major reduction of expenses, it does make education more accessible.

Engaging the Conversation as a Case Study

In order to engage the conversation about online education in this essay, I would like to describe and assess my own online course. I organize my description and assessment around the framework and methodology of a case study (see Carroll, 1986). Richard Davies describes case studies as "descriptions of phenomena, such as groups, events, classes, and institutions" (1984, 27). The method of case study

---

[2] According to our registrar and associate dean, Steve McLeod, if you include auditors the average age is 38 years old.

is often used to describe the unfamiliar or the unusual. Usually one thinks of such a methodology as studying people. I will use it, however, as a means of studying an inanimate entity, that is, online technology, and how students interact with it.

I adapt Nancy Vyhmeister's (2001, 145-149) four-fold process of a case study (observe, analyze, interpret, and act) to a three-fold process of observe, analyze/interpret, and act to organize this essay. First, I begin with observation. I will describe the phenomenon of the online environment and context. Second, I will assess (analyze and interpret) what I understand to be its strengths and weaknesses based upon my role as a participant observer and on the critique of other written resources. Third, Vyhmeister uses the word "act" to refer to future plans, strategies, and goals established in order to improve the experience. Since there is no set way to develop and structure an online course, I will provide only general strategies for proceeding forward for those who want to take the conversation further. I will offer brief suggestions for strengthening my own online class as well as ideas others might consider as they reflect on the online format. This structure provides an organized way of studying the online experience. I am not prescribing but describing and engaging in self-assessment. Hopefully this will serve to begin the difficult conversation.

Observation: Description of Context and Class

Harding School of Theology is a seminary associated with Churches of Christ located in Memphis, Tennessee. Our parent institution is Harding University located in Searcy, AR, which has a student population of about 4,855 (Burks, 2021). In the Master of

Divinity program one preaching class is required of all students. Students can choose from either Biblical Preaching or Sermon Development and Delivery to fulfill that requirement. The Sermon Development and Delivery class is the one I chose to put online.

My experience and exposure to online teaching has evolved over the years. Beginning in 2000, I used WebCT as a Learning Management System (LMS) in a rudimentary way, using a listserv to send out lectures in text form and students responding via the listserv. Preaching opportunities in class were limited to one sermon presentation per student when they came to campus for a single weekend. My initial experience and effort was below satisfactory. As a result, I did not offer the preaching class in an online format again until the fall of 2012. I have, however, taught a non-performance class, Congregational Ministry, online for over nine years. That class has almost been exclusively text based. I wrote out my lectures in narrative form and then uploaded them to the management system. Richard Ascough (2002), associate professor of New Testament at Queen's Theological College in Ontario, says this kind of instruction is nothing more than an outdated and expensive correspondence course.

The LMS Harding University used has also changed over the years: from WebCT to Blackboard, to Moodle, and then starting in the fall of 2013, to Canvas. Each LMS has required significant time to learn and to operate. Harding University has changed systems based on the efficiency of the system as well as its cost.

The fall of 2013 was the second time I taught Sermon Development and Delivery as a fully online class. The University limits the size of online classes to fifteen students. During the fall of 2012 there were fifteen students, but only six took it for credit. The rest were auditors.

During the fall of 2013 fifteen students took the class for credit. During the fall of 2014 I offered the class as a hybrid. However, in the fall of 2015 I was once again offering it as a fully online class. The course objectives of Sermon Development and Delivery included introducing students to current theories of homiletics, giving them opportunities to preach and receive constructive feedback, developing an approach to preaching that is holistic and not simply technique oriented, and understanding preaching as a spiritual discipline. During the first two semesters the class was offered fully online (Fall, 2012 and 2013), students were required to preach in chapel at least two times during the course of the semester and preferably three if the chapel schedule permitted. Students within three hours of campus were required to come to chapel on campus to preach. Those more distant students were required to submit two video sermons they preached in their congregations. Finally one weekend was required for all students to come to campus and preach one sermon before class members and the instructor.

The weekly layout of the online class began with a section entitled "Meditation Moment" which included a brief three to five minute video followed by a discussion forum designed to engage students in a time of reflection on their own spiritual development. One of the purposes of this component was to bring into the task of preaching the importance of one's own spiritual growth. Preaching is more than just learning theories and techniques. Preaching is a spiritual discipline. Therefore spiritual formation must be a part of the preaching discipline. Raewynne Whiteley (2008) is one among several who has championed this neglected area of preaching. The Meditation Moment section was one attempt to integrate personal spiritual formation into the curriculum. Another way was to ask students not only to critique the sermons they listened to throughout the course of the semester but also to identify how these sermons could influence their spiritual lives.

The next major section in the weekly structure I called the "Preaching Focus." This unit introduced and developed the particular topic to investigate for the week. Intermixed with this unit were discussion forums where students responded to the audio or video lectures I had recorded on Camtasia, a screen cast software, along with audio and video sermons to interact with and critique. A final section was the "Reading" component. Each week students read relevant articles and interacted with each other about those readings. I provided issues or questions that arose out of the articles for students to discuss and engage. Students were graded on these discussions, as well as on discussion forums located throughout the week's activities. This was the major framework for each week. The structure, however, was flexible and some components were added or deleted from the week's tasks depending on what was best needed to address the topic.

Assets of an Online Preaching Class

As I reflect on the benefits that have come with this class, one of the obvious is that offering the class online enables it to have a wider accessibility to individuals across the country. Over the two semesters I have offered it through this venue, students have enrolled from coast to coast, from Washington State to Boston and from Michigan to Louisiana. Students living overseas have also participated. In difficult economic times many students and preachers cannot disrupt their ministries or their careers or uproot their families and move to campus. The online class brings instruction to them. Those preachers and congregations, especially in remote regions of the country, benefit.

Since the average age of our student population is thirty-three years old, we are primarily educating adult learners. The online class enables students, especially adult students, to fit the class more easily into the routine of their weekly responsibilities. One student with three small children told me that he can best fit his school responsibilities in his schedule after his three grade school children have gone to bed.

Not only fitting with students' schedules, an online class can also adapt to the learning styles of adults. Kathleen Cercone (2008, 141) identifies some characteristics of adult learners in the following table.

Learning Styles and the Characteristics of Adult Learners

Learning Styles need to be considered. In any group of adults, there will be a wide range of individual differences, thus the individualization of learning experiences is important in many situations.

a. Ensure that students can move through the instruction at their own pace.
b. Ensure that the students can review previous learning whenever they want.
c. Provide links to a wide variety of web resources.
d. Ensure to allow ample time for students to master the content.
e. Ensure that all learning styles are addressed by presenting material in multiple modes including text, graphics, audio, and

        manipulatives.

f.   Use strategies such as consciousness raising, journal keeping, reflection logs, think sheets, and guided questioning.

I have found that the online presentation can adapt to these styles and enable adult learners to enjoy the learning process and learn more effectively. Visual learners are able to see videos of instructions and demonstrations. Auditory learners hear and critique sermons. Reading and writing learners engage in forum discussions. Finally kinesthetic learners have the opportunity to practice their preaching before peers.

In addition to these benefits, I have found that the online class forces me to reconsider how I teach and to think more creatively. It has brought freshness to a class I have taught for the past twenty-two years. I find myself using more media than I did in a traditional classroom. I am not limited to a three-hour session once a week. I can share these materials with students without taking time away from the lecture. The lectures are usually shorter and more succinct as I record them. I use Camtasia, to record my lectures adding slideshows, videos, images, and other media to better engage student viewers.

The online class has assisted me in interacting more with students and in bringing an important learning centered approach to the pedagogy (Long, 2008, 41-57). Students take responsibility to identify new insights and share perspectives with the rest of the class. As a teacher, I become more of a facilitator. Ascough (2002, 19) says, "Less control of the class is afforded the instructor in an online environment and the instructor becomes more of a facilitator or moderator. This loss of control can sometimes be disconcerting, but one must learn to adjust." I become less of a "sage on the stage" and more of a "guide on the side." The discussion forums have contributed greatly to enabling students to take more ownership of ideas shared. All students must contribute. No one can remain silent without entering into the discussion as they can in a traditional classroom setting.

The online class does provide visual and audio contact between students and teachers through several venues. One of these is a service like GoToMeeting, Zoom, or Google Meet. These enable students and professor to connect up in real time. The medium creates a virtual classroom that allows individuals to interact face-to-face at one time. Throughout the course of the semester, I require students to interact live at least three times. In addition, at the beginning of the semester students must introduce themselves via Canvas' built-in webcam. I also include two assignments that require students to respond via the VoiceThread tool. This medium threads in audio and video responses to the assignments for the class to watch. All of these media provide a variety of means to make visual contact between students and professors.

Interestingly, Ascough (2002, 19) points out that online learning reduces the potential for discrimination. He encourages thoughtful reservation regarding posting pictures and names of students believing there is an advantage to not knowing the age or ethnicity of other classmates. In support of Ascough's position, I have been told that some studies show that one of the reasons online dating (as an analog) works is because people derive primary associations from ideas and personalities and only secondarily associate people with their appearance. Delaying the requirement for visual interaction until several weeks into the semester might achieve the same goal with students, teaching them to associate names with ideas expressed in the forum rather than names with faces (and, consequently, gender, ethnicity, or race). I have found that the use of video media to communicate with students and between students, however, outweighs the advantage of not publicizing names or faces. Students going into ministry will minister in multi-ethnic contexts. They must learn to deal graciously with ethnic differences and what better way to do that than in a supervised context of online encounters?

Contrary to the legitimate concern that some raise about forming community online, community can be formed. I have discovered that students find it easier to share their spiritual and moral struggles online than they do in a traditional classroom. Fellow classmates almost always respond with grace and support when hearing of those struggles. Students find it enjoyable chatting and conversing with one another online. Forming community is important to the process of learning. D. Randy Garrison and Heather Kanuka (2004, 99) make the observation that students who feel a stronger sense of community are better able to move progressively through more difficult phases of critical thinking. Online learning has strong potential for creating a collaborative learning environment. The discussion forums are the most common means of interacting with students. They provide students with opportunities to give thoughtful and reflective responses to the lectures, readings, and sermons for which they are responsible.

Even though these are a few of the assets I have come to realize in teaching an online preaching class that problems, issues, and concerns also abound which makes the conversation difficult. Dialogue, however, can open the door for new insights and opportunities.

Challenges Facing an Online Preaching Conversation

As I mentioned in the opening paragraph, Delamarter (2005b) identified concerns raised about online education from faculty in theological seminaries across the country—twenty-six concerns in all! I have experienced and realized some of those concerns. One of them is the steep learning curve involved in adapting to the new technology. I have been slow and reserved, even resistant, to doing online courses. I have no technology background. So learning the technology has taken time and a lot of one-on-one training. Every change the University makes in choosing a new LMS results in having to take time to learn the system. I also have had to take time to learn new software and tools to use in the class. Among others, these include tools like GoToMeeting, Camtasia, and Voice Thread. This was one of the concerns Delamarter surfaced among seminary faculty. He discovered that the "experience of most people has been that the people who commit themselves to technology are committing themselves to learning curve after learning curve" (Delamarter, 2005b, 132).

With each new piece of software faculty must take time to learn and in addition expect to have to learn more when updates and changes are made. The learning curve also creates problems for students. Though some in the younger generations learn new technology quickly, others do not, which then creates pedagogical issues. To teach an online class effectively also imposes an additional burden on faculty; it usually takes more time to teach and manage online instruction than it does to teach in a traditional setting. Ascough (2002, 27) describes the time involved in the following way:

Since online course delivery is still very much in its infancy, particularly in theological schools, it is important that the faculty member(s) appointed to teach online seriously consider what it takes. At the very least, it takes extra time and effort to design and deliver an online course. Some suggest that it is at least fifty   percent more work than teaching in the classroom; some put the figure at three times more work (my own experiences suggest the latter figure is more likely the case at first). While this should not discourage faculty from accepting online course teaching assignments, they should be cognizant of the effort required (and hopefully compensated adequately).

One concern not mentioned, at least explicitly, in Delamarter's list was the potential for abuse by educational institutions. Some institutions attract students to online courses by advertising how quick and easy it is to get a degree. These institutions become nothing more than degree factories. Of course, degree factories were around before online courses came on the scene. Now, however, through the Internet, these degrees are easier and even more accessible. In response, since the fall of 2013, the federal government requires institutions (i.e., each professor) to calculate the number of hours each class offered requires of students. This applies not only to online classes but also to on campus classes.

In addition to these general problems with online education, preaching classes present the unique challenge of giving students opportunities to preach and receive feedback from peers and instructor. This is where the conversation becomes most difficult. The experience of preaching before peers and instructor is an essential component to offering preaching classes or for that matter any performance class. There are several ways of meeting this critical requirement in an online class. In the past the following scenario was the way I chose to ensure that this critical element of the preaching class was not overlooked. Students within three hours of driving distance were required to come to campus and preach in chapel twice during the course of the semester on the particular theme assigned for that school year. They were also to preach on the weekend that all students were required to come to campus. Those who lived more than three hours away were required to preach twice in a congregation where they attended or where they ministered, video record those sermons, and then send them to the instructor. On some occasions I required students to preach a live sermon on GoToMeeting. This is like preaching to a camera (in this case a webcam), but as they preach students do see the faces of their peers on the screen looking back at them. Though less than a desirable format, live online has value. Distant students, especially those overseas, benefit from hearing their peers preach and from receiving immediate feedback about their sermons.

Action: Future Direction for Online Preaching Classes

For those of us who have entered the online pedagogical conversation and want to continue to explore its value, we need to explore how online preaching classes can be improved. I am planning to make a few changes to my online course. First, with the approval of the administration, I am admitting only distant students (those beyond three hours of driving distance from campus) to the online class. This means that those who are not distant students will have to take the course on campus.[3] Second, with approval from the administration, I am limiting enrollment to no more than ten students. Enrollment limitation in the past was fifteen. The smaller enrollment will enable both students and instructor to maximize our time together. Third, in order to minimize the loss of the value of the face-to-face experience of preaching before peers and instructor and critiquing those sermons, I am requiring all distant students to preach a ten-minute sermon in front of a congregation or small group of listeners, video record that sermon, and submit it to me in digital form through the LMS. I will then assign three or four students, in addition to myself, to provide constructive feedback to the student. Students will submit two video recorded sermons.

Also as this difficult conversation moves forward, I want to briefly offer a few general items to keep in mind. Patricia D. Wolf (2006) argues for the importance of formally training faculty to teach online courses. Faculty members need to have a minimum level of computing skills, understand and manage the delivery system or the LMS (Blackboard, Canvas, Moodle, etc.), implement proper pedagogical methods, be involved in the course design, have institutional support, and possess a strong motivation to teach online.

Another perspective to keep in mind is that online blended learning is not just tacking on technology to a traditional classroom. It is about integrating the two. Garrison and Kanuka describe the task in the following way:

---

[3] Institutional requirements have changed since the writing of this chapter. Now, HST provides online live access to most courses.

To paraphrase Marshall McLuhan, it is not enough to deliver old content in a new medium. We must seriously reflect on how to design and deliver higher education. With the limited results of higher education in facilitating critical thinking (King & Kitchener, 1994), and the need for these abilities in our information age, it is becoming clear that it is essential we do better at facilitating critical, creative, and complex thinking skills. Blended learning offers possibilities to create transformative environments that can effectively facilitate these skills (Garrison and Kanuka, 2004, 99).

Those who choose further to explore the possibilities of online pedagogy will find there is no stereotypical online class that one can cut-and-paste into their system. While we should take opportunities to learn from others who have developed online classes, in the end instructors must adapt and customize what they do and how they develop the class to match their specific seminary context and constituency. We should also take opportunity to read other quality resources that will help give us a better understanding for creating a healthy online learning environment. Resources that have helped me in this process include Killacky (2011), Delamarter (2005a), Sajjadi (2008), and Hege (2011). However we build our online classes and the degree to which we use Internet sources with them, instructors should never allow technology to drive their pedagogy. In this regard Ascough (2002, 21) provides an important perspective: "What I am suggesting is that we need to put pedagogy before technology. The computer and all that it can do should be at the service of the teaching process."

Teaching performance classes online in theological seminaries poses special challenges. Some will decide such a medium is inappropriate and impossible. Others will find it as a new opportunity for enhancing the pedagogy of our discipline. What I hope this essay does is at least to stimulate further conversation regarding the value and the limitations of such an enterprise. Let the difficult conversation continue!

References

Ascough, R. S. (2002). Designing for online distance education: putting pedagogy before technology. *Teaching Theology and Religion,* 5(1), 17-29.

Carroll, J., Dudley, C., and McKinney, W. (1986). *Handbook for congregational studies.* Nashville, TN: Abingdon Press.

Cercone, K. (2008). Characteristics of adult learners with implications for online learning design. *Association for the Advancement of Computing in Education Journal,* 16(2), 137-159.

Davies, R., (1984). *Handbook for doctor of ministry projects: An approach to structured observation of ministry.* Lanham, MD: University of Press of America.

Delamarter, S., (2005a). Theological educators, technology and the path ahead. *Teaching Theology and Religion,* 8(1), 51-55.

Delamarter, S. (2005b). Theological educators and their concerns about technology. *Teaching Theology and Religion,* 8(3), 131–143.

Garrison, D. R., and Kanuka, H., (2004). Blended learning: Uncovering its transformative potential in higher education. *Internet and Higher Education,* 7, 95-105.

Hege, B. R., (2011). The Online theology classroom: Strategies for engaging a community of distance learners in a hybrid model of online education. *Teaching Theology and Religion,* 14(1), 13-20.

Killacky, C., (2011). Developing a useful teaching delivery selection model for theological seminaries using technology as a medium. *Journal of Adult Theological Education,* 8(2), 166-185.

Burks, D. (2021, February 1). Re: Enrollment [Electronic mailing message].

Sajjadi, S. M., (2008). Religious education and information technology: Challenges and problems. *Teaching Theology and Religion,* 11(4), 185-190.

Vyhmeister, N. J. (2001). *Quality research papers for students of religion and theology.* Grand Rapids, MI: Zondervan.

Whiteley, R. J., (2008). *Steeped in the holy: Preaching as spiritual practice.* Chicago: Cowley Publications.

Wolf, D., (2006). Best practices in the training of faculty to teach online. *Journal of Computing in Higher Education,* 17(2), 47-78.

2

Compensation and Ownership: The Current State of Online Course Development at Christian Colleges[1]

Rebecca Hoey and Fawn McCracken

Introduction

Online courses and programs have become a mainstream option offered by many American institutions of higher education. As institutions mature in their online operations, faculty concerns continue to evolve. Research from 2000-2009 revealed that one of the most significant motivators and barriers to faculty participation in online programs was fair compensation for online course development and teaching. Similarly, research from that time period reflects alarm by faculty as institutions began to assert ownership of courses developed for online programs. More current studies suggest practices have shifted to incentivize online course development and

---

[1] From "Compensation and Ownership: The Current State of Online Course Development at Christian Colleges," by R. Hoey and F. McCracken, 2015, NET: An e-Journal of Faith-Based Distance Learning. Reprinted with Permission. See distancelearningdirectors.org.

institutions have developed clearer course ownership policies. However, little has been published regarding specific ranges of compensation, common course ownership policies, and even less about whether a relationship exists between faculty participation, compensation levels, and ownership policies.

Institutions with less history offering online programs may lag behind in policies related to online course development compensation and ownership than their more progressive peers. As a sector, nonprofit private colleges have trailed after public and for-profit colleges in offering online options. Many private nonprofit colleges with membership in the Council of Christian Colleges & Universities (CCCU) did not offer their first fully online program until 2009 (Hoey, McCracken, Gerrett and Snoeyink, 2014). CCCU institutions are representative of their sector, as private nonprofit institutions with online offerings doubled between 2002 and 2012 (Allen and Seaman, 2013). However, nonprofit private colleges had not yet reached the percentage of online programs in 2012 that public and for-profit colleges offered a decade earlier (Allen and Seaman, 2013).

In 2014, 70% of college administrators reported that online education was critical to their strategic plan (Allen and Seaman, 2014), and the recent surge of online programs at CCCU institutions suggests that college administrators at nonprofit private institutions share this direction. The purpose of this research, then, was to answer the following questions regarding the state of course ownership and compensation for online course development at private non-profit Christian colleges affiliated with the Council of Christian Colleges and Universities:

1. What is the current state of course development, compensation, and ownership for courses developed for online programs at CCCU institutions?

2. Is there a relationship between faculty involvement in new online program development and institutional policies related to ownership?

3. Is there a relationship between whether faculty are compensated for course development and institutional policies related to ownership?

4. Is there a difference in the number of programs offered by institutions who share ownership of online courses with their faculty? (i.e. Are faculty more motivated to develop courses for programs when ownership is shared?)

The findings of this research may guide college administrators at nonprofit private Christian colleges to develop policies on course ownership and compensation that result in optimal outcomes for strategic growth and faculty satisfaction.

Literature Review

The responsibility for new course development has long been held by the faculty, as has the implied ownership of those courses. This tradition was logical, as the course and the faculty member were difficult to separate; the syllabus and tests could be shared with another faculty member, but the actual instruction could not. Changes in the past two decades brought about by the growth of online learning have challenged the custom of faculty ownership. The development model for new courses has shifted to include teams comprised of not just faculty but instructional designers and media specialists (Borgemenke, Holt and Fish, 2013; Hoyt and Oviatt, 2013). All materials required for learning are packaged digitally and are easily transferable. Faculty members have more direct venues to profit from courses they develop including selling their work to third-party vendors and offering their courses directly to consumers in MOOCs. This may result in a conflict of interest and even direct competition with the institution for which the faculty course developer is employed (Domonell, 2013). These changes have resulted in some institutions' asserting ownership of online courses and programs (Blanchard, 2010; Domonell, 2013; Hoyt and Oviatt, 2013; Kranch 2008).

Legally, copyright belongs to the creator of a work unless the work was created as a part of an employee's employment—called the work for hire doctrine. However, the "teacher exception" to work for hire may give teachers copyright protection of the course materials they develoAccording to the federal legislation Restatement (Second) of Agency, a court may evaluate ownership of course materials using this three part test: whether "1) it is of the kind of work [the employee] is employed to perform; 2) it occurs substantially within authorized work hours, and 3) it is actuated, at least in part, by a purpose to serve the employer" (City of Newark v. Beasley, 1995). The second criteria related to work hours has become murkier to distinguish as personal and work life blend—particularly for faculty who may work at least occasionally from home using online technologies (Johnson, 2014).

Though court cases challenging ownership have gone both ways, the institution may have more legal right to ownership of a course than the developer if the developer was an employee teaching within an online program as part of their regular employment (Blanchard, 2010). In the case of work for hire, the institution needs no special agreement or contract with an employee to claim ownership of the course (Rosini, 2014).

Despite the legal implications of course ownership, colleges and universities must consider their institutional culture and the motivation of their faculty to participate in the development of courses for online programs when determining matters of course ownership, The American Association of University Professors (AAUP) asserts that institutions and faculty should work together to ensure faculty have control over their scholarship (Springer, 2005). The most equitable solution may be an agreement negotiated between the faculty and institution that gives shared ownership rights to the institution and the faculty course developer (Blanchard, 2010; Johnson, 2014; Kranch, 2008; Rosini, 2014).

In a recent national survey of administrators at 110 doctorate-granting research universities, Hoyt and Oviatt (2013) found that 84% of institutions either had an intellectual property policy in place or were developing one. Those policies give more ownership rights to the institution; 41% of respondents indicated joint ownership of courses, 36% indicated institutional ownership, and only 10% allowed faculty to retain full ownership of courses they developed as part of their employment. Regardless of who retained ownership, faculty at institutions with a policy in place or in development were more willing to create an online course than those at institutions where no policy existed.

The Hoyt and Oviatt (2013) research also revealed that 82% of responding institutions compensated faculty for online course development. The high percentage of institutions that incentivized course development may reflect an acknowledgement of faculty concerns about compensation from the previous decade.

In a National Education Association (2000) survey on distance education, two-thirds of the 534 college faculty respondents expressed concern that they would not be fairly compensated for their intellectual property. Similarly, Muilenburg and Berge (2001) surveyed more than 2500 college administrators, faculty and staff and found faculty compensation among the highest ranking barriers to distance education, particularly to faculty at institutions new to distance education.

Insufficient compensation was also a barrier reported in research by Belcheir and Cucek (2002), Haber and Mills (2008), Chen (2009), and Lloyd, Byrne and McCoy (2012). These concerns were not unfounded. A survey of 152 institutions (Schifter, 2004) revealed that faculty overload pay was among the least likely expenses paid for online course development. Extrinsic rewards including additional salary, course releases, and course stipends are a primary motivator for faculty to participate in online education (Cook, 2012; Hoyt and Oviatt, 2013), particularly those without experience teaching online (Betts and Heaston, 2014; Lloyd, Byrne and McCoy, 2012).

While compensation and ownership are widely cited as barriers, the inarguable growth of online programs in the last decade (Allen and Seaman, 2014) suggests either growth is happening at institutions who have addressed faculty concerns, or these barriers do not actually prevent faculty from developing online courses. Harvard faculty members receive no compensation for developing online courses for the virtual learning platform edX (Fu, and Zhang, 2015). Orr,

Williams and Pennington (2009) found faculty appreciated compensation received for online course development but would have developed online courses even if no compensation had been provided. Survey research by Green and Alejandro (2009) revealed the opportunity to participate in course development was a significant factor in retaining faculty who teach online. Outside of the research of Hoyt and Oviatt (2013), little if any research is available to determine whether relationships exist between faculty involvement, course ownership policies, and level of compensation for course development.

There were also few published data on specific compensation policies related to online course development. Without hard numbers it may be challenging for institutions to determine a fair market rate of compensation. What is available reveals a significant range of compensation and a variety of different formulas for compensation. Schifter's (2004) survey of 152 intuitions revealed overload pay for course development ranged from $0-$7500 with a mean range of $1620-$2470. Burleson's (2011) survey of 161 institutions revealed that 59.6% provided financial compensation for course development with a range from $0 to $10,000 and a mean and mode of $1001-$2500. Linardopoulos's (2012) evaluation of 12 universities revealed a range of online course development compensation from $0 to $16,000. The Instructional Technology Council's (2014) online survey of 71 ITC member institutions found that 54.9% compensated faculty for course development with a range of $0 to more than $5000, with most respondents indicating an amount between $501 and $3000. None of the studies suggested a consistent compensation structure based on credits, flat rate, or other form.

Institutional policies for course ownership and compensation are in flux but appear to trend toward more significant institutional ownership and more compensation for faculty course development. Hoyt and Oviatt's (2013) research provided a solid, current survey of the field but given the different level of publication, invention, research, and faculty control between doctorate-granting research institutions and nonprofit private Christian colleges. A difference may exist in policies addressing ownership .As well, nonprofit private colleges may be less represented in surveys related to compensation from the past 15 years as they have less history with online learning (Allen and Seaman, 2014; Schifter, 2004). This research was necessary to inform the work of college administrators related to online course ownership policies and course development compensation at nonprofit private Christian colleges.

Method

Participants

The population of interest in this research was the 120 nonprofit private Christian college and university members of the Council of Christian Colleges & Universities (CCCU). CCCU institutions are counted among the 1600 private nonprofit institutions in the United States, 900 of which have religious affiliation. All institutions with membership in the CCCU are regionally accredited, and most are four-year comprehensive colleges and universities. CCCU institutions are located in 32 states and serve more than 300,000 students (CCCU Profile, 2014).

Survey

Researchers developed a survey that consisted of 56 questions. The questions were intended to collect descriptive data regarding enrollment, number of programs, administrative structure, administrator, efficiency, oversight, governance, job duties, faculty involvement, course compensation, course ownership, and professional development for online programs. Findings on academic structures and the current state of online education at CCCU member institutions were published in the *Online Journal of Distance Learning Administration* (Hoey et al., 2014). Beyond descriptive institutional data, this study was based on the following survey questions:

- Are faculty responsible for developing courses in online programs?
- [If no, then] Who develops courses for online programs?
- Are faculty compensated for course development for online programs?
- [If yes, then] How are faculty compensated?
  - Stipend
  - Course release
  - Either stipend or course release
  - Other
- What is the amount of the stipend?
- Who owns the course after it is developed?
  - Faculty member who developed the course
  - Institution
  - Joint-ownership is shared

- My institution has no policy regarding course ownership
- Please indicate the areas facilitated by the third-party vendors:
  - Instructional Design
  - Course Development
- For each statement below, indicate the level to which the traditional faculty are involved with online programs. (No involvement, some involvement, full involvement)
  - New online program proposals
  - New online program development
- Does your institution have a separate division for online or adult programs?
  - Yes
  - Somewhat
  - No
- The survey was digital and was developed using the online survey program Qualtrics. Survey responses are confidential, and maintained in Qualtrics by Northwestern College.

Procedures

An invitation to participate with the link to the digital survey, was sent to the email addresses of the administrators responsible for the online programs at 107 of the 120 CCCU institutions on February 10, 2014. The invitation to participate was sent to the provost or chief academic officer at institutions where no online program administrator was apparent. Direct email addresses for administrators at 10 of the CCCU institutions were not found, and 3 email addresses resulted in undeliverable communication.

In addition to the initial invitation, reminder emails were sent to prospective participants on three occasions before the survey closed 18 days after opening. As well, an announcement was placed on the CCCU listserv for chief academic officers, and another regarding the research and survey was made to provosts and members of the Commission on Technology who attended the Council of Christian Colleges & Universities: Engaged Community conference in Los Angeles, California.

Descriptive statistics were conducted on data collected using measures of central tendency including range, median, and mean. The inferential statistic conducted to describe relationships between dichotomous variables was the chi square tests of association. An alpha of p = .05 was used to determine significance for all statistical tests.

Findings

This study examined the current state of course development, compensation and ownership of online courses at CCCU institutions. The following research questions guided the study:

1. What is the current state of course development, compensation, and ownership for courses developed for online programs at CCCU institutions?
2. Is there a relationship between faculty involvement in new online program development and institutional policies related to ownership?

3. Is there a relationship between whether faculty are compensated for course development and institutional policies related to ownership?
4. Is there a difference in the number of programs offered by institutions who share ownership of online courses with their faculty?

Of the 107 survey invitations emailed to administrators of online programs, 59 responses were received generating a 55.1% response rate. To determine whether respondents reflected the total population of CCCU institutions, enrollment in online programs for the respondents was compared with enrollment in online programs of all CCCU institutions using data obtained from the Integrated Postsecondary Education Data System (IPEDS). There was no significant difference between the number of students enrolled in online programs among respondents (M = 361.33, SD = 682.27) and the number of students enrolled in online programs in the population (M = 342.85, SD = 859. 07), F(1, 134) = 0.016, p = 0.90. Respondents were representative of the population with respect to enrollment in online programs. However, the 45% of CCCU institutions who chose not to participate may have different characteristics, including no enrollment in online programs, different policies on ownership of online courses, and different practices on compensation for the development of online courses.

The survey was completed by 28 provosts, 14 deans, 16 directors, and one unknown position. In this study 91.5% (n = 54) of respondents reported their institution offered at least one fully online, hybrid, or low residency program that contained online courses. The findings presented below were based on those 54 respondents.

Faculty Involvement in Online Course Development

Survey participants were asked to assess the level of involvement of traditional faculty members in new online program development. Out of 43 participants who responded to the question, it was found that 14% (n = 6) of institutions had no traditional faculty involvement in new online program development, 40% (n = 17) had some involvement, and 46% (n = 20) had full involvement of the traditional faculty in developing new online programs.

In this study, 63% (n = 34) of institutions with online programs reported that faculty were responsible for developing online courses in online programs. Nine institutions (17%) indicated their courses were developed by the following: instructional coordinators, online program chairs, content experts, programmed packaging, faculty or content experts with a design team, the dean, or online course developers. Eleven respondents (20%) provided no response to questions pertaining to course development.

Course development was facilitated by a third party vendor at nine institutions, and eight institutions utilized a third party vendor for instructional design. Six of the institutions that used a third party for course development also reported that faculty were responsible for course development. This may mean that some courses were developed by a third party and others by faculty, or that faculty were still utilized in some capacity in the design and development of online courses.

Online Course Development Compensation

Of the 34 institutions where faculty were responsible for course development, 91% (n = 31) provided additional compensation to faculty for their work in course development. Compensation included a stipend (n = 16) or a combination of stipend and course release (n = 14). One respondent indicated a design contract, which may assume monetary compensation.

When compensation was provided as a stipend, the compensation amount ranged from $500.00 to $4000.00 per course. Some institutions (n = 12) offered a flat rate that ranged from $500.00 to $2000.00 per course with the median and mode both being $1000.00 per course. Some institutions (n = 9) compensated based on the course credits or length of the course. In this model, four institutions paid $500.00 per credit hour and one institution paid $250.00 per week of the course. Other institutions (n = 6) noted the compensation varied between $500 and $4000 but did not provide an explanation of the factors that contributed to the variation.

Ownership of Intellectual Property

In this study, participants were asked "Who owns the course after it's developed?" The following options were provided to respondents: faculty member who developed the course, institution, joint-ownership is shared, and my institution has no policy regarding course ownershiThere were 44 responses to this question with 26 (59%) indicating the institution retained exclusive ownership, 15 (34%) indicating joint-ownership, and three (7%) indicating no policy regarding course ownership (See Figure 1). None of the respondents indicated that the faculty member who developed the course retained sole ownership of the intellectual property.

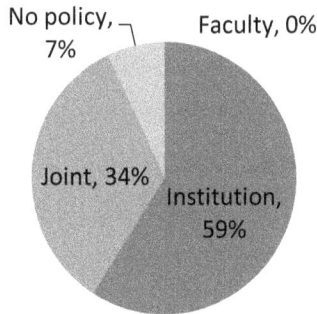

Figure 1. Pie chart depicting the party that retains ownership of online courses developed for online programs.

Faculty Involvement, Compensation, Course Ownership, and Online Programs

Beyond describing the current state of course ownership and compensation, research questions guiding this study led to examination of potential relationships between faculty involvement in online course development, online course ownership, and compensation for online course development at private non-profit Christian colleges. One of those questions was whether the institutional policy on who retained ownership of an online course was related to how willing faculty were to become involved in online course development. Using a chi-square test of association, it was found that there was no statistically significant association between faculty involvement and ownership of online courses, X^2 (4, N=43) =

1.59, p = .81. That is, faculty participation in the development of new online courses was not related to whether faculty retained ownership rights to courses they developed.

Similarly, this study attempted to uncover a potential relationship between faculty compensation for course development and institutional policies related to ownership. Researchers were interested in determining whether institutions that provided compensation for course development were more or less likely to claim or share ownership of online courses. Using a chi-square test of association it was found that there was no statistically significant association between faculty compensation and ownership of online courses, X^2 (2, N=34) = 2.54, p = .28. This may be due to the fact that faculty were almost always compensated for course development regardless of who retained ownership of the course and that faculty never retained sole ownership of the online courses in this study.

This study also investigated whether institutions that had faculty-only or joint-ownership policies had more online programs than institutions that retained institutional ownership of courses. Though number of programs may not be the direct result of faculty motivation, number of programs may be influenced by the faculty's motivation to participate in online course development and online programming. The variables of interest were the possessor of ownership rights (the faculty who developed the course, the institution, a joint ownership agreement, or no policy in place) and the number of online programs at the institution. Institutions that participated in this study reported offering between 1 and 96 online programs. Forty-two institutions responded to both survey questions regarding total number of programs and ownership of online courses. Those institutions were classified into three categories based on the total number of online programs: small (1-4 programs), average (5-10 programs), and large (greater than 10 programs). Given those classifications, 48% (n = 20) of institutions were classified as small, 31% (n = 13) of institutions were classified as average, and 21% (n = 9) of institutions were classified as large (See Table 1). Using a chi-square test of association, it was found that there was not a relationship between the number of online programs offered at the CCCU institution and the ownership policy for online courses, X^2 (4, N=42) = 2.31, p = .68. As participants in this research reported that faculty developed online courses in online programs, and the number of online programs was not related to the type of course ownership policy, it may be inferred that faculty at participating institutions were not more or less likely to develop online courses if they were assured of sole or joint ownership.

Table 1

Ownership Rights	Number of Online Programs			
	Small	Average	Large	Total
Faculty	0	0	0	0
Institution	10	8	6	24
Joint	8	5	2	15
No policy	2	0	1	3
Total	20	13	9	42

Discussion

The purpose of this research was twofold: to determine the current practices for course development compensation and ownership of online programs at nonprofit private colleges who were members of the Council for Christian Colleges & Universities (CCCU) and to uncover any relationships related to course ownership, compensation, and number of online programs. A review of the literature provided current research on this topic from doctorate-granting institutions (Hoyt and Oviatt, 2013). Many member institutions of the CCCU do not offer online doctoral programs, and the literature was sparse on nonprofit private Christian colleges. This is particularly important as nonprofit private colleges have a shorter history of offering online programs (Allen and Seaman, 2013; Hoey et al., 2014), which may mean their policies and culture are different.

This study revealed marked similarities between practices for course compensation and ownership at CCCU institutions and institutions noted in the literature. In research conducted by Hoyt and Oviatt (2013), 84% of doctorate-granting institutions either had an intellectual property policy in place or were developing one. Per those policies, 36% of institutions retained exclusive ownership of online courses, 41% of institutions shared joint ownership with the faculty course developer, and 10% allowed faculty to retain full ownership of courses they developed as part of their employment. In this research, 93% of institutions indicated a policy; 59% of institutions retained exclusive rights and 34% shared joint ownership. Not one institution responding to this survey allowed faculty to retain exclusive ownership of online courses.

Similarly, research conducted by Hoyt and Oviatt (2013) revealed 82% of responding institutions compensated faculty for online course development. In this study, 91% of responding institutions did the same. These statistics appear to reflect a shift in practice from a decade prior, when faculty overload pay and release time were among the least likely expenses paid for online course development (Schifter, 2004).

As with other studies that reported specific compensation for online course development (Burleson, 2011; Hoyt and Oviatt, 2013; Linardopoulos, 2012; Schifter, 2004), compensation paid for online course development at institutions who participated in this research varied both in structure and amount. However, patterns emerge from the body of literature. Institutions in this research and others commonly paid a flat rate compensation for course development, or they paid per unit/credit hour. Regardless of the structure, an amount between $1000 and $2500 was common in this research, similar to that reported by Schifter (2004), Burleson (2011), and the Instructional Technology Council (2014). However, compensation at CCCU institutions in this study ranged from $0 - $4000. The compensation range reported by Burleson of $0 - $10,000 (2011), Schifter of $0 - $7500 (2004) and Linardopoulos of $0 - $16,000 (2012) suggests compensation at CCCU institutions varies less widely and has a lower top level, particularly given that Schifter's research was conducted a decade prior.

Faculty at institutions who participated in this research were involved in new online program development with 86% reporting some or full involvement. Involvement commonly included course development; 79% of institutions reported that their faculty were responsible for course development, even when the institution also reported they used third-party vendors for course development or instructional design. Of the remaining 21% of institutions that did not indicate faculty were responsible for course development, faculty were still at times included in teams that developed new online courses.

Most surprising, though, was the apparent lack of negative impact from joint and even exclusive institutional ownership of online courses on total number of programs. Faculty were no less likely to be involved in course development at institutions where the institution claimed ownership of the courses they developed, and no more likely to develop for institutions where they retained joint ownership. Similarly, institutions that retained full ownership had no fewer online programs than institutions that shared ownership of online courses developed for online programs. Given that the great majority of faculty at institutions in this study were involved in the development of online courses and programs, it appears ownership policies did not diminish their participation.

It should be disclaimed that faculty at institutions that participated in this research may have felt compelled to contribute to the development of online programs for reasons beyond the scope of this research—reasons more important to them than ownership and compensation. The development may have been a part of the faculty member's regular course load. The faculty member may have elected to contribute to the development of online programs to ensure academic rigor, quality, and faith integration similar to programs offered at their traditional onsite campus. Enrollment concerns may have necessitated the development of online programs in order to retain jobs.

Compensation may also be a contributing factor that explains why course ownership policies had no impact on the number of online programs at participating CCCU institutions or the number of faculty participating in course development. Nonprofit private colleges have a shorter history offering online programs (Allen and Seaman, 2013), and faculty with less experience teaching online are generally more motivated by the extrinsic reward of compensation than intrinsic rewards like meeting the needs of students who are unable to attend class on campus (Betts and Heaston, 2014; Muilenburg and Berge, 2001). At 91%, almost every institution that participated in this research reported compensating faculty for their work in course development—either in the form of stipends or course releases. As almost every institution provided compensation, there was no relationship to suggest institutions exchanged compensation for full institutional ownership.

Implications for Practice

The percent of faculty members receiving compensation for the development of online courses at CCCU member institutions rivals that of faculty members receiving compensation at other colleges and universities. Stipends and course releases for online course development, the forms of compensation offered by the CCCU institutions in this study, reflect the type of extrinsic incentives that encourage faculty participation in the online course development process (Cook, 2012). One area that may be evaluated by CCCU institutions is the top end amount of monetary compensation offered for the development of online courses. The monetary compensation received for developing online courses at CCCU institutions is at the lower end of the compensation range found in other studies (Schifter, 2004; Burleson, 2011; Linardopoulos, 2012), which may deter faculty in programs that traditionally earn a higher salary. CCCU institutions are encouraged to offer competitive monetary compensation rates for the development of online courses because they appear to be closely linked with faculty motivation to participate in online course development.

The number of institutions in this study that reported a policy related to the ownership of online courses is impressive. Given that 38 percent of institutions within the Council of Independent Colleges (CIC) are still experiencing issues related to ownership of intellectual property (Clinefelter and Magda, 2013), it was a bit surprising that only three institutions in this study do not have a policy in place related to the ownership of intellectual property. Over the past decade it has become a best practice for institutions to develop a policy related to ownership of intellectual property in online courses. Institutions are encouraged to continue to use the literature related to ownership of intellectual property in online courses as policies are revised and written.

Suggestions for Future Research

Given the limited literature on compensation for developing online courses, a better understanding of compensation methods and amounts could be beneficial in understanding faculty engagement in online course development. Does one method of compensation prove to be more beneficial than another method of compensation? A larger study of monetary compensation amounts from both public and private institutions would also be helpful in future research.

A substantial percentage of public and private institutions share joint ownership of online courses with faculty developers, but research is lacking that provides commonalities and ramifications of the specific arrangements for shared ownership. A plethora of questions emerge when considering joint-ownership policies. What does joint-ownership between individual faculty members and institutions entail? When there is joint-ownership of online courses, are there royalties associated with these online courses? If the jointly owned course becomes a master course within an online program, how much revision can be made to the course without consultation with the original course developer? Continued research needs to be conducted to better understand joint-ownership of online courses in this age of continued growth of online programs.

Conclusion

Private nonprofit Christian colleges may have less history offering online courses and programs than their public and for-profit counterparts, but institutional members of the Council of Christian Colleges & Universities do not lag behind in policies of intellectual property rights for ownership of online courses or compensation practices for course development. In this research, faculty elected to develop courses for online programs when they shared ownership of those courses and when their institution claimed exclusive rights. That may be attributed to the fact that almost every responding institution that relied on faculty for course development also compensated faculty for their work. CCCU member institutions averaged a similar compensation amount of $1000 - $2500 for course development compared to other institutions, but the range of $0 - $4000 was lower than the range of $0 to as high as $16,000 reported in other research. However, the literature remains sparse on research that widely reports details of compensation for online course development. This and other research suggests institutions of higher education have responded to faculty concerns from 2000-2009 regarding fair compensation for online course development and that institutions have indeed significantly increased their claim of ownership of intellectual property for online course development. Future research should focus on the most effective structures for compensation, the market rate for compensation of online course development, and specific details of policies related to joint and full institution ownership of online courses developed by faculty. It is certain these issues will increase in importance as more private nonprofit Christian colleges commit to a full cadre of online programs.

References

Allen, E. and Seaman, J. (2013) Changing course: Ten years of tracking online education in the United States. Retrieved from http://www.onlinelearningsurvey.com/reports/changingcourse.pdf

Allen, E. and Seaman, J. (2014) Grade change: Tracking online education in the United States. Retrieved from http://www.onlinelearningsurvey.com/reports/gradechange.pdf

Belcheir, M. and Cucek, M. (2002). Faculty perceptions of teaching distance education courses. Research Report 2002-02. Retrieved from http://files.eric.ed.gov/fulltext/ED480925.pdf

Betts, K and Heaston, A. (2014) Build it but will they teach? Strategies for increasing faculty participation and retention in online and blended education. *Online Journal of Distance Education 17*(2). Retrieved from http://www.westga.edu/~distance/ojdla/summer172/betts_heasto n172.html

Blanchard, J. (2010). The teacher exception under the work for hire doctrine: Safeguard of America freedom or vehicle for academic free enterprise? *Innovative Higher Education, 35*(1), 61-69.

Borgemenke, A., Holt, W., and Fish, W. (2013). Universal course shell template design and implementation to enhance student outcomes in online coursework. *Quarterly Review of Distance Education, 14*(1), 17-23.

Burleson, J. A. (2011). Faculty compensation for developing and delivering online courses. *ProQuest LLC.*

CCCU Profile (2014). Retrieved from http://www.cccu.org/about/profile.

Chen, B. (2009). Barriers to adoption of technology-mediated distance education in higher-education institutions. *Quarterly Review of Distance Education, 10*(4), 333-338.

City of Newark v. Beasley. (1995). 883 F. Su3 (D.N.Y.). Retrieved from http://law.justia.com/cases/federal/district-courts/FSupp/ 883/3/1767270/

Clinefelter, D. L. and Magda, A.J. (2013). Online learning at private colleges and universities: A survey of Chief academic officers. Louisville, KY: The Learning House, Inc.

Cook, R. (2012). Facts and fiction: Lessons from research on faculty motivators and incentives to teach online. In *E-Learning-Engineering, On-Job Training and Interactive Teaching* (Chapter 5). Retrieved from http://cdn.intechopen.com/pdfs-wm/ 32042.pdf

Domonell, K. (2013). The rights question. *University Business*, 16(5), 44-46.

Fu, M. and Zhang, Z. (2015). Making classes, but not money. The Harvard Crimson. Retrieved from http://www.thecrimson.com/article/2015/5/28/faculty-edx-experience/

Green, T. and Alejandro, J. (2009). The retention of experienced faculty in online distance education programs: Understanding factors that impact their involvement. *The International Review of Research in Open and Distributed Learning, 10*(3).

Haber, J., and Mills, M. (2008). Perceptions of barriers concerning effective online teaching and policies: Florida community college faculty. *Community College Journal of Research and Practice, 32*(4-6), 266-283.

Hoey, R., McCracken, F, Gehrett, M., and Snoeyink, R. (2014). Evaluating the impact of the administrator and administrative structure of online programs at nonprofit private colleges. *Online Journal of Distance Learning Administration, 17*(3). Retrieved from http://www.westga.edu/~distance/ojdla/fall173/hoey_ mccracken_gehrett_snoeyink173.html

Hoyt, J. and Oviatt, D. (2013). Governance, faculty incentives, and course ownership in online education at doctorate-granting universities. *American Journal of Distance Education, 27*(3), 165-178.

Instructional Technology Council (2014). ITC quick poll results – Special faculty compensation and training for distance education. Retrieved from http://www.itcnetwork.org/resources/itc-quick-polls/916-itc-quick-poll-results-special-faculty-compensation-and-training-for-distance-education.html

Johnson, D. (2014). Who owns that course? *Educational Leadership, 72*(2), 83-84.

Kranch, D. A. (2008). Who owns online course intellectual property? *Quarterly Review of Distance Education, 9*(4), 349-356.

Linardopoulos, N. (2012). Faculty compensation for online courses: A revised approach. *The University of Fraser Valley Research Review, 4*(2). Retrieved from http://journals.ufv.ca/rr/RR42/article-PDFs/5-linardopoulos.pdf

Lloyd, S., Byrne, M., McCoy, T. (2012). Faculty-perceived barriers of online education. *Journal of Online Learning and Teaching,* 8(1).

Muilenburg, L and Berge, Z. (2001). Barriers to distance education: A factor-analytic study. *American Journal of Distance Education, 15*(2).

National Education Association, W. D. (2000). A survey of traditional and distance learning higher education members. Retrieved from http://files.eric.ed.gov/fulltext/ED445571.pdf

Orr, R., Williams, M., Pennington, K. (2009). Institutional efforts to support faculty in online teaching. *Innovative Higher Education, 34*(4).

Rosini, N. (2014). What's a work-for-hire and why should you care? *The Chronicle of Higher Education*. Retrieved from http://chronicle.com/article/Whats-a-Work-for-Hire-and/150333/?cid=atandutm_source=atandutm_medium=en

Schifter, C. (2004). Compensation models in distance education: National survey questionnaire revisited. *Online Journal of Distance Learning Administration* 7 (1): 1–14. Retrieved from http://www.westga.edu/~distance/ojdla/spring71/schifter71.pdf

Springer, A. (2005). Intellectual property legal issues for faculty and faculty unions. American Association of University Professors. Retrieved from http://www.aaup.org/issues/copyright-distance-education-intellectual-property/faculty-and-faculty-unions-2005

3

Online Doctoral Students at a Faith-Based University: Concerns of Online Education[1]

Kelly Price, Julia Price, and Deborah Hayes

Introduction

Online doctoral degrees are in higher demand than ever (Fuller, et al., 2014). The number of students expected to earn online doctoral degrees is expected to grow (Evans and Green, 2013). As online education becomes more respected and accepted, the working professional is able to access an advanced degree while benefiting from the flexibility online education provides (Offerman, 2011). Over half of online doctoral program students are enrolled part-time and are often professional practitioners who have served many years in their field (Gardner and Gopaul, 2012). Many of these professional practitioner online doctoral students seek efficiency and customization of research interests (Green and McCauley, 2007). Berry (2017) found

---

[1] From "Online Doctoral Students at a Faith-Based University: Concerns of Online Education," 2018, NET: An e-Journal of Faith-Based Distance Learning. Reprinted with permission. See distancelearningdirectors.org.

that online doctoral students indicate cohort, class groups, small peer groups, and study groups help them feel an increased sense of community. Therefore, it may be posited that the interests of students seeking an online doctoral degree are exceptionally varied.

Jove (2015) found that in online doctoral programs, practical projects assist in leadership development, including "scholarship, stewardship, social interpersonal skills, and self-concept." Numerous online doctoral students note criteria on which they base their satisfaction regarding the online learning experience. One study found that this included work-academic balance, support, and sense of belonging (Garder and Gopaul, 2012). Even gender plays a role in the online doctoral environment. Rockinson-Szapkiw (2017) found that women have more confidence in completing an online doctoral degree if there is the support of an influential advisor, such as an employer, and supportive reference groups. Therefore, attributes sought in an online doctoral program are diverse and possibly complex in nature.

Several studies have noted the most prevalent concerns of doctoral students when enrolled in an online doctoral program. Some have anxiety over not feeling a sense of community or feeling isolated (Yuan and Kim, 2014; Jairam and Kahl, 2012). Others have concerns over the dissertation process, student to instructor relationship/interaction including feedback, research pressures, employment/finding a job/salary, quality of training, and student experiences such as individual development, support and flexible delivery (Jones, 2013). Some doctoral students experience concern with technological/computer-related problems while others state that instructor behavior influences overall dissatisfaction with online doctoral learning (Bolliger and Halupa, 2012).

Even though these studies have been conducted within numerous areas of online doctoral education, few have focused on the specifics of online doctoral education in a faith-based university or institution. Thus, the purpose of this study is to supplement the literature in this area and to provide information to those faith-based institutions who currently offer, or will offer online doctoral degrees in the future.

Literature Review

Faith-Based Online Education

Approximately 1000 institutions in the United States identify with having a religious affiliation (Council of Christian College and Universities, 2017 and StateUniversity.com, 2017). Faith-based organizations and institutions are developing more online educational programs as the online student population increases (Rogers and Howell, 2005). Additionally, many students seeking a faith-based education are considering online programs and courses to advance their education (Carnevale, 2006). Some faith-based organizations concluded that they should not offer online programs until the online environment was proven effective and the materials were proven to be quality. However, these obstacles have been resolved by advances in online learning (Rogers and Howell, 2004.) Rovai and Baker (2004) found that students at a faith-based university felt a deeper sense of community among distance and traditional platforms than students at a comparable secular university.

Further, one of the main tenets on faith-based education is the care for the whole student which includes not just academic development but moral and spiritual developments, as well (Rovai et al., 2008). One unique aspect of faith-based education in the higher education environment is that educators see themselves not only as role models for their students, but also as faith-mentors (Woodson, 2010) even in the online environment. In other words, the whole person is considered within online platforms and the structure of the classes are developed as such. Another study (Olson, 2011) found that faculty, cultural diversity, and student relationships are a few of the important variables that have a significant impact on student spiritual development. However, while faculty at faith-based institutions try to reach students on many levels, some faculty think online education is slightly enhanced at the graduate level (Hall, 2015) while also caring for the whole person. Some Christian higher education institutions have questioned the effectiveness of online learning, citing that it cannot possibly address the whole person or allow for spiritual growth. Conversely, as Lowe and Lowe (2010) found, distance education programs can provide spiritual formation through online learning communities "regardless of physical proximity." Currently, faith-based institutions offer online chapel services, virtual prayer rooms, a virtual table and other communities in which to address the whole person and spiritual growth (Maddix and Estep, 2010) in the online environment. These offerings could be viewed as attractive options to the student seeking an online education in the faith-based environment.

Faith-Based Doctoral Programs

Faith-based doctoral programs have received some attention in the literature. For example, a faith-based doctoral degree, "can be used as a driver of leadership while also incorporating rigorous research standards for the dissertation" (Forman, 2016). However, faith-based dissertations are often completed with the student's having no religious affiliation when making the choice of dissertation topic (Lunde, 2017). Additionally, being a faith-based institution requires unique teaching methods and poses unique questions. For example, one of these questions is, how does a faith-based instructor "affirm a student's faith and encourage a coalescence of their personal beliefs and professional practice" (Anderson, 2014)? Another unique question for faith-based online teaching is "How can a biblical studies course encourage adults to use their imaginations in ways that are both playful and productive for learning?" (Delamarter et al., 2011). Even questions such as how to facilitate deep spiritual formation in the online environment and how to maximize that effort has been posited in faith-based online learning research (Flynn, 2013).

Based on the literature, it can be said that doctoral online education is a mainstay in the education learning environment and that faith-based institutions are realizing and developing online programs at many levels, including the doctoral level. It has also been noted that with online education several unique challenges, not related to traditional learning environments, can occur. More specifically, online doctoral education brings additional concerns and challenges, such as the dissertation process and instructor relationships (i.e. proposal defense via video chat with professors one has never met in the physical environment). Furthermore, faith-based online doctoral education programs bring some of the same challenges and include the challenging and/or rewarding variable of spiritual growth and educating the whole person.

Methods

The purpose of this study is to address student concerns of faith-based online doctoral education. It is the intent to discover the most prevalent student concerns regarding this specific type of education and to discover if these concerns varied from non-faith based online doctoral program concerns found in the literature. The primary objective of the survey was to assess student concerns within an online doctoral program and to determine if adjustments needed to be made to the program as a result of the responses.

The research was conducted at a small, private faith-based university in the United States. The survey was sent in Fall 2016 via email to all new students entering the doctoral program, which was a total of 60 students. A total of 28 students (majority female) returned useable surveys via email (51% return rate). To ensure anonymity, the departmental graduate advisor sent and received all the emails and gave the researchers the results with no student names attached to the survey.

The fourteen-item survey instrument was constructed of items reflecting information regarding student online concerns found in two sources. The first source of relevant information was found in the professional literature related to student concerns with online learning. The second source of pertinent information was gathered via student inquiries received by the researchers while teaching online courses. Inter-rater reliability was conducted regarding the survey. Fourteen statements (as shown in Table 1) were included to which students responded to a 5-point Likert scale of numerical value, indicating a range of *very concerned (1)* to *not concerned (5)*. An opportunity for open response or comments was also included.

Results

Concerns given in the survey were: communication between student and professor, technology knowledge regarding use of the course management system, rigor of courses, internet access, professor engagement, isolation, advising, assignment quality, course design, professor quality, workload, personal time requirements, preparation for dissertation, and completion of degree in timely manner.

Participants were not concerned with items 4 (internet access), 10 (professor quality), 2 (technology knowledge regarding the use of the course management system), and 8 (assignment quality). They were slightly concerned with items 7 (advising), 1 (communication between student and professor), 6 (isolation), 9 (course design), 5 (professor engagement), 3 (online rigor of courses) and 14 (completion of the degree in a timely manner). However, when asked to rate work load, (item 11), personal time requirements (item 12), and preparation for dissertation (item 13), students were more concerned (Table 1).

Table 1

Student Concerns

Item Number	Item	Median	Mean
4	Internet access	5	4.93
10	Professor quality	5	4.43
2	Technology knowledge regarding use of the course management system	5	4.43
8	Assignment quality	5	4.29
7	Advising	4.5	4.25
6	Isolation	4	4.14
1	Communication between student and professor	4	4.25
9	Course design	4	4.07
5	Professor engagement	4	4.04
3	Online rigor of courses	4	3.64
14	Completion of degree in timely manner	4	3.46
11	Workload	3.5	3.21
12	Personal time requirements	2.5	3.04
13	Preparation for dissertation	2.5	2.75

The anecdotal comments provided by candidates supported the findings on the Likert scale questions. Item 13 addressed concerns regarding the dissertation preparation. For example, one participant responded, "My main concern is preparing for the dissertation. This is my only drawback to an online program over a face-to-face program." Another candidate reported, "I have had no communication concerning the preparation for dissertation. I am unsure if that occurs now or later; however, I would like to start thinking about it and wrapping my mind around the requirements in plenty enough time." While the respondents addressed item 12 by expressing concern over the time requirements necessary to complete the online program, one student put the issue into perspective. The participant stated, "I have found that the professors I have had thus far are very accessible and helpful. I appreciate the timely and effective feedback given after assignments are submitted. I am slightly concerned about the dissertation preparation, work load, and time requirements, but I feel comfortable with the support given. I know that everyone is willing to help." Item 1 was found in a response that stated, "My biggest concern is communication. I am afraid of missing important information since I'm not on campus. Having another form of email to check is also a concern."

Conclusions

The results revealed several interesting conclusions. First, there are some differences between faith-based and non faith-based online doctoral students' concerns. Faith-based students were not as concerned about being isolated or about professor interaction and technology issues as were non faith-based students, as indicated by the professional literature. This may be due to the fact that most of the students in this program use technology on a daily basis within their jobs as well as interaction with colleagues. However, both types of students were very concerned with the dissertation. This may be due to the unfamiliarity of the process and perceptions regarding the major undertaking of a dissertation.

Second, some unique themes surfaced with further analysis. Although the doctoral program is 100% online, technology (internet access and technology usage) was found to be an area of minimal concern. Students may already be confident in this area. Most students are working professionals who use technology daily. Also, students were not concerned with quality issues (professors and assignments). Further research could be conducted to investigate if these items were of no concern due to university reputation, trust in the program, positive word-of-mouth or additional reasons.

When observing items that fell in the middle of student concerns (items 1, 3, 5, 6, 9 and 14), one may find that they each relate to working independently, which inherently results in a domino effect or causal relationship among those middle items. For example, it could be argued that bad or ineffective advising could lead to a feeling of isolation or that the students felt they are "on their own" while making their way through the program. If they felt isolated, this could lead to a worry or anxiety about the program components such as the courses (rigor or design) and professors (communication or engagement). Thus, those worries could compound into a concern about completing the degree in a timely manner.

When noting the items for which students indicated the most concern, the commonality was time issues. These include preparation for the dissertation, personal time requirements and workload. Those students drawn to online programs are also ones who tend to be working full time or have other obligations (Radford, 2011). Therefore, enrolling in an online doctoral program may alleviate time issues that surround going to a physical classroom or having class at a specific time or location.

Recommendations

Based on the results and further analysis, three recommendations are offered. First, the same students could be surveyed again with the same survey at the mid-point of the program. This would allow researchers and administrators to observe any changes in the mindset of the student after having spent some time in the program. Students could also be surveyed at the end of the program for the same reason. Additionally, it could be recommended that adjustments be made to the program based on the findings. For example, more information may be added to a student guide regarding the dissertation process and time expectations. Finally, administrators could use the findings to market the program to achieve marketing objectives. Strategies could be used to attract students based on their concerns and how the program can address and help them achieve their goals despite these obstacles and concerns.

While this study addressed only one faith-based university, the results could benefit many faith-based institutions with online doctoral programs. Being able to determine student primary concerns prior to their entrance to an online doctoral program at a faith-based university may allow for several competitive advantages in regard to competing against other faith-based and secular online doctoral programs. First, more successful and efficient marketing campaigns could be developed. Whether using traditional tactics such as print or television or using digital means like social media or email, programs could tailor messages to counteract any initial concerns the student may have about dissertation preparation, time requirements and/or workload. Another benefit seen by the faith-based program could be the more effective initial engagement with potential students. If caring for the "whole person" is a focus of the faith-based education process, as indicted by the literature, then faculty, advisors, staff, and administration could collaborate to ensure the potential students feel this engagement on a level not seen at secular institutions. Finally, the faith-based online program could benefit by realizing increased retention and graduation rates via proactively nullifying areas of high concern to alleviate apprehension of pursuing the faith-based online doctoral degree.

References

Anderson, T. (2014). Teaching professional ethics in a faith-based doctoral program: Pedagogical strategies. *Journal of Psychology and Theology, 42*(1), 164-173.

Berry, S. (2017). Student support networks in online doctoral programs: Exploring nested communities. *International Journal of Doctoral Studies, 12.*

Bolliger, D. and Halupa, C. (2012). Student perceptions of satisfaction and anxiety in an online doctoral program. *Distance Education, 33*(1).

Carnevale, D. (2006, April 28). Many religious students look to distance education. *The Chronicle of Higher Education, 52.*

Council for Christian Colleges and Universities (CCCU). (2017). About CCCU. Retrieved from http://www.cccu.org/about

Delamarter, S., Gravett, S., Ulrich, D., Nysse, R. and Polaski, S. (2011). Teaching biblical studies online. *Teaching Theology and Religion,* 14(3), 256-283.

Evans, T., and Green, R. (2013). Doctorates for professionals through distance education. In M. G. Moore (Ed.), *Handbook of Distance Education* (3rd. ed, 654-669). New York, NY: Routledge.

Flynn, J. (2013). Digital Discipleship: Christian education in a digital world. *Christian Education Journal,* 10(1), 88-89.

Forman, L. (2016). Examining the perceptions and effectiveness of a faith-based university's doctoral program. Retrieved from ProQuest Dissertation and Theses database. (UMI number: 10140143)

Fuller, J. S., Risner, M. E., Lowder, L., Hart, M., and Bachenheimer, B. (2014). Graduates' reflections on an online doctorate in educational technology. *Techtrends: Linking Research and Practice to Improve Learning, 58*(4), 73-80.

Gardner, S. K., and Gopaul, B. (2012). The part-time doctoral student experience. *International Journal of Doctoral Studies, 7.* Retrieved from http://ijds.org/Volume7/IJDSv7p063-078Gardner352.pdf

Green R, and Macauley, (2007). Doctoral students' engagement with information: An American-Australia perspective. *Libraries and the Academy, 7,* 317-332.

Hall, D. (2015). Resistance, reluctance and revelation: Examining faculty perceptions of online learning options at a faith-based university. Retrieved from ProQuest Dissertation and Theses database. (UMI number: 3702130)

Jairam, D. and Kahl Jr, D. (2012). Navigating the doctoral experience: The role of social support in successful degree completion. *International Journal of Doctoral Studies, 7,* 311-329.

Jones, M. (2013.) Issues in doctoral studies – forty years of journal discussion: Where have we been and where are we going? *International Journal of Doctoral Studies, 8.*

Lowe, S. and Lowe, M. (2010). Spiritual formation in theological distance education: An ecosystems model. *Christian Education Model, 7,* 1, 84-102.

Lunde, R. (2017). Predicting dissertation methodology choice among doctoral candidates at a faith-based university. Retrieved from ProQuest Dissertation and Theses database. (UMI number: 10266092)

Maddix, M. and Estep, J. (2010). Spiritual formation in online higher education communities: Nurturing spirituality in Christian higher education online degree programs, *Christian Education Journal, 7,* 2, 423-434.

Offerman, M. (Spring, 2011). Profile of the nontraditional doctoral degree student. *New Directions for Adult and Continuing Education.* 129, 21-31. Wiley Periodicals.

Radford, A. (2011). Learning at a distance: Undergraduate enrollment in distance education courses and degree programs. *U.S. Department of Education.* Accessed from
 http://nces.ed.gov/pubs2012/2012154.pdf

Rockinson-Szapkiw, A., Spaulding, L. and Lunde, R. (2017). Women in distance doctoral programs: How they negotiate their identities as mothers, professionals and academics in order to persist. *International Journal of Doctoral Studies, 12.*

Rogers, C. and Howell, S. (2004). Use of distance education by religions of the world to train edify and educate adherents. *The International Review of Research in Open and Distributed Learning.* Accessed from: http://www.irrodl.org/index.php/irrodl/article/view/207/290

_____. (2005). Religious Institutions and distance learning. In Ed. Mehdi Khosrow-Pour. *Managing Modern Organizations with Information Technology.* Vol. 2. Hershey: Idea Group Publishing.

Rovai, A. P., and Baker, J. (2004). Sense of community: A comparison of students attending Christian and secular universities in traditional and distance education programs. *Christian Scholars Review, 33*(4), 471-489.

Rovai, A., Baker, J., and Cox, W. (2008). How Christianly is Christian distance education? *Christian Higher Education, 7*(1), 1-22.

StateUniversity.com. (2017). Colleges and universities with religious affiliations –Characteristics, relationships, leadership and control, issues for the future. Accessed November 3, 2017, from http://education.stateuniversity.com/pages/1860/Colleges-Universities-with-Religious-Affiliations.html

Woodson, S. K. (2010). *Cura personalis* in online undergraduate Christian higher education. Retrieved from ProQuest Dissertation and Theses database. (UMI number: 3390690)

Yuan, J., and Kim, C. (2014). Guidelines for facilitating the development of learning communities in online courses. *Journal of Computer Assisted Learning, 30*(3), 220-232.

4

An Investigation into the Implications of Dewey's "Learning Situation" for Online Education[1]

Timothy Paul Westbrook, Morgan McGaughy,
and Jordan McDonald

Introduction

While the tools of technology upgrade almost daily, educators are left with the daunting task of integrating digital progress with educative principles. As technology continues to provide new tools, course designers and subject matter experts have the responsibility to look beyond "the latest thing" and to evaluate the new instruments' usefulness for learning. Given the more established place of online learning in higher education (Legon and Garrett 2017, 10), the burden

---

[1] From "An Investigation into the Implications of Dewey's 'Learning Situation' for Online Formation,' 2018, <u>Net: An eJournal of Faith-Based Distance Learning</u>. Reprinted with permission. See distancelearningdirectors.org.

for supporting digital innovation with educational principles has also become more crucial.

At the heart of online learning program development, educators face the epistemological dilemma of whether they are to use the Internet for the redistribution of knowledge (perennialism) or to use the Internet to provide access to knowledge (constructivism/ progressivism). Although programs may select combinations of these two, at the end of the day, administrators must decide if they are willing to invest in learning models that lead students to construct, engage, and experience knowledge. Otherwise, their sophisticated technology may do nothing more than transmit information from one device or computer to another with expectations that somewhere along the way students also upload the information to their brains. In order to avoid a simple information transfer, course designers ought to build into online courses ways for learners' experiences to become part of the curriculum.

John Dewey recognized the significant role real-life experiences play on learning. Dewey drew from Romantic philosophers, such as Rousseau, Pestalozzi, and Froebel, and applied their principles of sensory experience to his twentieth-century American context (Dewey, 1916). His aim was to explore ways of learning for the benefit of education as a discipline (Dewey, 1938). As institutions of higher learning bring online academics toward the mainstream of education, they should consider how Dewey's principles of experience apply to today's context. The purpose of this article is to invite distance educators to consider how Dewey's understanding of learning by experience affects online course design. In order to explore the role of experience in online learning, this study conducted a phenomenological analysis of student experiences from an online course. The analysis was guided by the following research question: "In what ways does the interaction of past experiences and present community impact learning online?" The student feedback revealed *flexibility*, *travel*, and *communication* as important themes that support Dewey's "learning situation" as a theoretical framework for experiential learning online.

Related Literature

A growing body of recent literature on distance learning emphasizes the importance of social learning and interaction in online education (see Thor et al., 2017; Howell et al., 2017; Westbrook, 2015). Carver, King, Hannum, and Fowler (2007), by focusing on experiential e-learning (or eelearning), introduce important concepts for joining experience and learning at a distance, such as "learner-centric," "agency," and "belongingness." They suggest a six level taxonomy for experiential e-learning: type 1 "content sharing," type 2 "online conversation," type 3 "meaningful online conversation," type 4 "drawing on student experiences," type 5 "problem-based/service learning," and type 6 "direct experience/action learning." The authors conclude that "the addition of concepts from experiential education can bolster e-learning environments," especially given that experiential e-learning helps students overcome some of the challenges of learning in isolation (Carver et al., 2007, 255). Following their lead, Baasanjav (2013) overlays Kolb's Experiential Learning Theory onto these "eelearning core concepts" and applies this integration of theory to an online course design. Bartley (2006, 23) calls for assessment strategies that are "interactive and engaging." Collins and Halverson (2009) promote the "lifelong-learning era" that echoes the progressive movement of the twentieth century in light of innovative developments in computer technology. They write, "The pedagogy of the lifelong-learning era is evolving toward reliance on interaction..." (97). Conrad and Donaldson (2004), drawing from the work of Dewey, Bruner, Vygotsky, and Piaget, insist that online pedagogy incorporate social constructivism in order to avoid courses' becoming merely "digital correspondence" courses (6). Koontz, Li, and Compora (2006) write, "The implementation of a constructive environment online can be done through the process of discovery learning.... This constructive approach is necessary in Web-based instruction because students are forced to access, retrieve, reconstruct, adapt, and organize information in a way that is meaningful to their learning" (27). Mason and Rennie (2008) point toward interactive interfaces and "connectivism" as the way forward "for learners to flourish in a digital era" (19). It should come as no surprise that progressive modes of delivery utilize progressive theories of education. The challenge for the road ahead will be for online enthusiasts to ground innovative design with objective assessment and theoretical exploration.

Cassady and Mullen (2006) explore electronic field trips (EFT) as a means to enhance the learning experience for online students. They report how Ball State University, in conjunction with institutions such as The Smithsonian Institute and National Aeronautics and Space Administration (NASA), has created EFTs that incorporate live broadcasts, simulations, online games, discussion boards, and teaching materials. The design of the EFTs creates a learner-centered environment, following a constructivist model. Cassady and Mullen (2006, 151) evaluate the EFTs by implementing Bruce and Levin's (1997, 82-91) adaptation of Dewey's (1900, 59-61) natural impulses of learning ("inquiry," "communication," "construction," and "expression"). They conclude that these impulses provide a taxonomy that helps administrators in distance education create a "coherent framework" for resource selection and EFT design (Cassady and Mullen, 2006, 159).

Addressing the problem that not all students everywhere have access to elite museums and research centers, the EFT experiment successfully demonstrates how an interactive museum experience open to all students via the Internet generates natural inquiry, allows for educative communication, and lends itself to constructive learning. However, the study also recognizes how the gap in time and space for asynchronous learners limits the efficacy of EFTs in the construction and expression domains (Cassady and Mullen, 2006, 157-160).

While images alone may conjure emotive inquiry from students, visual representation does not replace the full sensory experience of physically being at a site. In one example, the authors describe how students' watching high-definition imagery of the Grand Canyon conjures similar responses to the monument as a personal visit would. Although the Grand Canyon's beauty may be enjoyed on video or in pictures, an experience of the Grand Canyon limited to audio and video is not the full Grand Canyon experience. A picture or even motion picture does not come close to the sensation of one's standing on the rim trail with amazement and realizing that her or his senses cannot absorb the canyon's width and depth. While computer programmers continue to improve "sensory-filled experiences"

(Wagner, 2006, 49), a simulated experience merely imitates the in-person experience.

In contrast to digital field trips, study abroad programs actually place students in 3-dimensional laboratories in which the students are experiencing new cultures, languages, and historical sites. Savicki's (2008) multi-authored book provides studies in which students in these study abroad programs document their learning of intercultural competency from real-time and real-life experiences. Selby writes, "...study abroad students experience something that is truly *transformational*" (2008, 1). While students personally process intercultural experiences, the faculty on the trip offer "purposeful intervention" that helps students make the most of their overseas learning encounters (Lou and Bosley, 2008, 282). The interest of this current study is to explore the role of experience and online education, and, as is described below, several of the participants were taking an online class about culture while attending study abroad programs. The connection, then, is to consider how both face-to-face encounters and digital learning environments may be bridged as experiential resources for learning.

Lowe and Lowe's (2010) application of Bronfenbrenner's (1979) ecology of human development to distance education offers the framework for considering this bridge between digital connections and one's personal face-to-face interactions. Intending to address the American Theological Society's (ATS) standards for spiritual formation in distance programs, Lowe and Lowe suggest that distance education courses draw from students' greater social network for transformation and learning. They write, "Ecological diversity, whether biological, social, or spiritual, creates an enriched environment that stimulates beneficial interaction among living organisms similar to the sapiential observation that 'iron sharpens iron, as one person sharpens another' (Prov 27:17, Today's New International Version)" (Lowe and Lowe, 2010, 90).

Comparing the ecological environment to a set of nested Russian dolls, Bronfenbrenner suggests four systems that envelop an individual's development: the microsystem, mesosystem, exosystem, and macrosystem. He describes the most immediate connections or interactions with others as the microsystem (Bronfenbrenner, 1979, 22). The mesosystem he describes as "interrelations among two or more settings in which the developing person actively participates" (25). The exosystem includes events, activities, and settings that have an effect on an individual though he or she is not an active participant (25). The macrosystem comprises a collection of the three lower systems that form continuities, or "consistencies," at the subcultural or cultural level (26).

Lowe and Lowe (2010, 93) regard the interaction, or inter-connectedness, in Bronfenbrenner's theory as helpful to envisioning successful online learning. The term "connection" has obvious links to online education; indeed, the Internet has taken interconnectedness to a new dimension. Lowe and Lowe (2010, 98) correctly point toward the students' ecological environment as a resource for learning, noting how one's family, church, and community provide social interaction that has educative value. As distance educators and administrators design and implement online curricula, they ought to give careful thought to how each student can perceive his or her immediate surroundings as possible sources of social learning and enhanced sensory perception, thus moving away from the real-world versus school-world separation (Roberts, 2007, 225).

A form of education that integrates online and face-to-face learning is blended learning, an integration that approaches a paradigm for applying Dewey's educative experience with distance education (Graham, 2006, 3). Garrison and Vaughan (2008, 17-29) speak of the community of inquiry that grows out of three types of presence: social presence, teaching presence, and cognitive presence. Social presence online exists when course participants project themselves authentically into online space through forums, blogs, or in other forms of communication. Teaching presence joins content and design with the scaffolding of the facilitator. Students also participate in the teaching presence when they make valuable contributions to discussions. One may describe the cognitive presence as the "aha" moments, meaningful exchanges, measurable integration of course materials, and other events where learning occurs. These three overlapping domains comprise the educational experience, resulting in a community of students and teachers engaged in inquiry and learning.

While all three of these domains may exist in pure face-to-face and online courses, both modes of delivery have different strengths. Garrison and Vaughan (2008) write, "It is our experience that the communication media do have different advantages. Therefore, educators need to consider which phases of an educational task are best conducted in an online or face-to-face environment" (37). To use social presence as an example, while online discussions lend themselves to a safe, trusting environment for students to explore deep thinking, face-to-face collaboration tends to result in higher levels of interaction (Hawkes and Romiszowski, 2001, 287). A well-designed blended course, then, consists of elements for face-to-face collaboration as well as online forums for individual and student-to-student reflection.

John Dewey's View of Experience

A tendency for education historically has been to create a dichotomy between traditional and student-centered models of learning. John Dewey, however, advised against "either-or" approaches to education (Dewey 1938, 21). At a time when traditional curriculum was challenged by utilitarian impulses (Cremin, 1961, viii), Dewey's appeal provided balance between information exchange and real world application. In his classic history of the Progressive Movement, Cremin acknowledges the lasting effects left by these efforts:

... granted the collapse of progressive education as an organized movement, there remained a timelessness about many of the problems the progressives raised and the solutions they proposed.... The Progressive Education Association has died, and the progressive education itself needed drastic reappraisal. Yet the transformation they had wrought in the schools was in many ways as irreversible as the larger industrial transformation of which it has been part (1961, 352-353).

One cannot deny the ways the Progressive Movement transformed American schools. With the incorporating of a holistic approach to curriculum, the influence of social science theories, and initiatives to reduce social class bias in the school system, today's students and teachers stand on the shoulders of theorists and practitioners who sought a better way to teach children in a democratic society.

The Post-Enlightenment era and Romanticism created a climate in which innovators such as Rousseau, Pestalozzi, and Froebel would develop learner-centered models of education. However, other forces of the times, such as the Industrial Revolution, immigration, urbanization, and poverty, stifled child-centered education, leading toward a product-centered, or factory model. Thus, the old guard of tradition devalued learning by experience.

Toward the end of the 19th century, the growing pains of a developing nation rekindled interest in education that was practical and accessible to the working class and immigrants. For example, Francis W. Parker undertook a reform of the Quincy, Massachusetts, schools. According to Cremin, Dewey regarded Parker as the "father of progressive education" (1961, 21). In 1893, Joseph Mayer Rice challenged traditional schools with his book *The Public-School System of the United States* (Rice, 1893; see Reese, 2001). Educators in this movement took seriously social concerns, and its leaders revisited school systems as a means to "Americanize" the children of the working class and immigrants in proper manners, in ethics, and in pursuit of American democracy (see Cremin 1961, 66-89). Shapiro writes, "No symbol of humanitarianism was more meaningful to progressives than childhood" (Shapiro, 1983, 171).

Effects of Progressivism could be seen ubiquitously. Gamson records Frank Cooper's initiatives in Seattle, Washington, from 1901 to 1922. Cooper encouraged the implementation of "active learning" and "creative play" (Gamson, 2003, 422). Wallace (2006) documents Angelo Patri's child-centered reforms in New York City during the Great Depression and leading up to World War II. In 1907 in Gary, Indiana, William Wirt developed a work-study plan that brought "hands-on" learning to traditional curriculum (Volk, 2005). It was during this era that philosopher John Dewey sifted through the period's cries and offered a balanced voice, assimilating learning by experience into a traditional system.

As a "pragmatic naturalist," Dewey addresses the paradigm shift that eighteenth century writers, such as Rousseau, brought forth (Eames, 1977; Noddings, 2012, 26). He writes, "The seeming antisocial philosophy was a somewhat transparent mask for an impetus toward a wider and freer society.... The emancipated individual was to become the organ and agent of a comprehensive and progressive society" (Dewey 1916, 59). He also credits Rousseau, Pestalozzi, and Froebel for originating the emphasis of natural education in early learning (Dewey 1916, 74). According to Dewey, natural education was a reaction against the Protestant doctrine of total depravity, where nature was regarded as God's work and social interference of God's divine plans was "the primary source of corruption in individuals" (1916, 73). Although Dewey regards this view as an oversimplification, he acknowledges the value of natural education's quest to overturn the powers of injustice when he writes, "It is the aim of progressive education to take part in correcting unfair privilege and unfair deprivation, not to perpetuate them" (1916, 76).

Dewey gleans from the experiential impulse of natural education: "An ounce of experience is better than a ton of theory simply because it is only in experience that any theory has vital and verifiable significance" (1916, 90). Dewey also writes, "In critical moments we all realize that the only discipline that stands by us, the only training that becomes intuition, is that got through life itself" (Dewey, 1900, 31). Learning from experience, then, begins with the senses of the student: "The senses—especially the eye and the ear—have to be employed to take in what the book, the map, the blackboard, and the teacher say" (1916, 88). The senses serve as "external inlets and outlets of the mind," conducting information exchanges between material objects and the mind (1916, 89). In Dewey's words, "To 'learn from experience' is to make a backward and forward connection between what we do to things and what we enjoy or suffer from things in consequence" (1916, 87-88).

If sensory perception leads to learning, then one would reason that learning experiences ought to focus on making sensory impressions. In *Experience and Education* Dewey certainly takes this view. He offers childhood recess as an example of children's learning rules for schoolyard games as they negotiate social guidelines (Dewey, 1938, 52-53). Reminiscent of Friedrich Froebel's kindergarten, Dewey writes, "The planning must be flexible enough to permit free play for individuality of experience and yet firm enough to give direction towards continuous development of power" (Dewey, 1938, 58; 2005, 135, 174). He even echoes Romanticism's sentiment on loose clothing as an aid to learning in this critique: "Strait-jacket and chain-gang procedures had to be done away with if there was to be a chance for growth of individuals in the intellectual springs of freedom …" (Dewey, 1938, 61; Froebel, 1906, 60, 63; Rousseau, 1979, 43). In other words, children learn through sensory perception, and prohibiting their movement, such as when bundling infants, limits their experiments and experiences with the world.

According to Dewey, education has an organic connection with students' experiences; yet not all experiences benefit the student, or in Dewey's terms, are "genuinely educative" (1938, 25). Experience alone does not educate; rather the depth of the learning depends on the quality of the experience. Dewey refers to this range of experiences as the "experiential continuum" (1938, 28). Even traditional education, he says, gives "a plethora" of experiences, but unless students achieve learning outcomes from those experiences, the unintentional, traditional exercise falls short of a quality educative experience (1938, 26). Dewey presents two criteria for an experience to be educative: continuity and interaction. An experience satisfies continuity when students adapt something from the past in a way that benefits the future (1938, 35). Interaction involves the individual or individuals who guide, facilitate, and scaffold learning (1938, 42). When continuity and interaction intersect, according to Dewey, a learning "situation" occurs (1938, 43).

Figure 1 illustrates how the learning situation results when one's interaction with the object to be learned intersects with the learner's experience. The vertical axis indicates the continuum between one's self-reflection and interaction with another person, place, or event. The greater the contact from facilitators, classmates, and individuals from one's context, the less students reflect in order to assimilate new information. The inverse is also true. The more students spend reflecting on their own, the less their learning includes feedback from others. The continuity of experience line indicates educative experiences from the past and anticipates experiences in the future. The arrows show how the learning situation does not occur only once, but rather repeats throughout one's intellectual growth (Roberts, 2007; see also Kolb 1984, 22-23). Depending on the subject matter and the needs of the students, the horizontal line moves up or down. The spiral illustrates the non-sequential and unpredictable nature of deep thinking.

While learning begins with the senses, an educative experience also requires reflection: "Thought or reflection ... is the discernment of the relation between what we try to do and what happens in consequence. No experience having a meaning is possible without some element of thought" (Dewey, 1916, 90). In order to direct reflection toward growth in understanding, Dewey suggests a five-step method for an intentional reflective experience rather than a trial-by-error approach to thinking, echoing the scientific method and anticipating the accommodation and assimilation components of cognitive stage-theory. The five steps are listed below the figure:

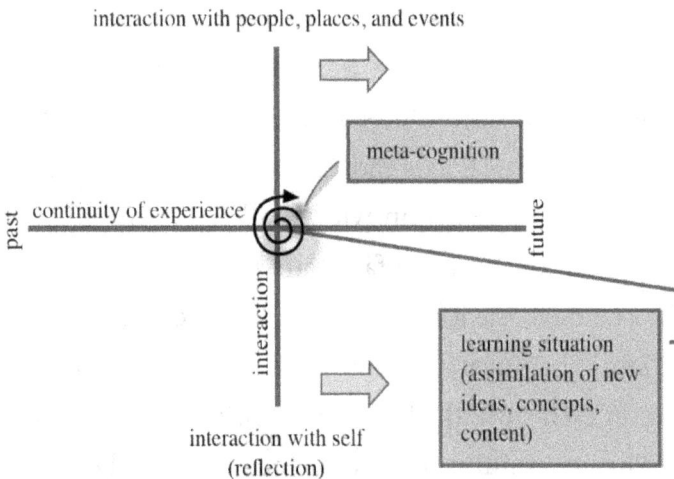

Figure 1. An Adaptation of Dewey's Learning Situation

1. "Perplexity, confusion, doubt, due to the fact that one is implicated in an incomplete situation whose full character is not yet determined."
2. "A conjectural anticipation—a tentative interpretation of the given elements, attributing them to a tendency to effect certain consequences."
3. "A careful survey (examination, inspection, exploration, analysis) of all attainable consideration which will define and clarify the problem in hand."
4. "A consequent elaboration of the tentative hypothesis to make it more precise and more consistent...."
5. "Taking one stand upon the projected hypothesis as a plan of action which is applied to the existing state of affairs: doing something overtly to bring about the anticipated result, and thereby testing the hypothesis." (Dewey, 1916, 93)

Thus, students reflect when they attempt to make sense of inconsistencies in their experiences (Dewey, 2005). Haphazard, trial-by-error reflection does not benefit student learning as much as intentional exploration of thought. Reflection with a purpose enhances thinking and creates ways for students to understand, apply, and own new content.

Dewey's concept applied to distance education helps course designers to evaluate their decisions when organizing content, creating online interactions, and exploring other ways for students to achieve learning outcomes. A forum post that encourages collaboration between students and facilitators would target a learning situation toward the middle of the interaction axis. Online journaling, intended to encourage self-reflection, would fall lower on the interaction line. For both forums and journals, carefully crafted prompts and questions are to summon student experience as a tool for understanding new concepts.

A century after Dewey challenged traditional education, causing educators to rethink how they write curriculum, teach, and value the child's role in the learning process, his theory continues to guide course developers in the digital age toward learning strategies that take into account how people think in addition to what content must be transmitted. Dewey's caution for balance remains timeless: "... it is not of new versus old education nor of progressive against traditional education but a question of what anything whatever must be to be worthy of the name *education*" (1938, 90).

Research Design

This current study applied Dewey's theoretical framework of continuity of experience and interaction to a phenomenological analysis of student learning online. A single online class from a private liberal arts university was selected. Although a single course as the primary source of data could be viewed as a limitation, the interest of the study was more focused on the intersection of experience and online learning than the actual case itself. Merriam (2009, 48) refers to this type of qualitative research as an "instrumental case study," in that the examination of a particular case provides information about a process that has transferable qualities beyond the case. By applying Dewey's "learning situation" to contextual matters of online learning, the following research question guided the data collection and analysis:

RQ: "In what ways does the interaction of past experiences and present community impact learning online?"

After obtaining permission from the Institutional Research Board of the participating university (kept on file), the researchers proceeded to identify the case for the investigation. They chose a single course from a private, liberal arts, faith-based school for the following reasons. First, the course contained learning outcomes that included intercultural competencies, which by definition suggested extra-course experiences. Second, this course had built into the design assignments that required reflection on lived experiences of the students. Third, the participating students were a blend of international students, adult learners in the United States, and U.S. American study-abroad students. The study examined the individual experiences of participants who were sharing in common educational activities that spanned across international locations. Confidentiality of participants was strictly protected throughout the process.

The selected course is taught online three times a year, and class size ranges from 10 to 40 students each term. The term selected for this study was in May-August of 2016 (considered to be the summer term of the university). Students in this course were both traditional-aged students as well as adult learners in non-traditional programs. Their ages ranged from 20-37, and there were a total of 33 students enrolled. As an online class, students participated from the main campus, from their home states, from their home countries (particularly from China), and from other countries in a study abroad program, which included campuses in Greece and Italy.

The researchers determined that this broad spectrum of

participation would allow for a variety of experiences by the students who shared a common learning space. Common themes shared by these students would then indicate phenomena that may be typical to learning situations in an online learning environment. In terms of transferability for a case study such as this one (Gall, Gall, and Borg 2007, 476; Patton 2002, 584; Lichtman 2013, 299-301), the common themes shared by these participants have applicability to the larger population of students who participate in online learning spaces with classmates located globally.

The researchers triangulated the data by analyzing through the lens of the research question the course participation and responses to a survey instrument developed by the researchers. Two specific online discussion questions were of interest. In one discussion question, students were told to "find one person from a culture other than yours and discuss with him or her what you are learning about worldviews...." In a second discussion question students were asked to discuss with a person outside of class about a particular topic relevant to their learning module. In both instances, the course assignments required outside interaction. Students' reflections in their discussion posts were considered as indirect data of how their experiences with others contributed to their learning online. The researchers reviewed a third course assignment that served the purpose of a summative assessment for the course. This assignment, based on problem-based learning models, required students to work in groups in order to create a five-year strategy for working in an intercultural setting. Not only did this assignment encourage interpersonal interaction, it also was assessed with the VALUE rubric for intercultural knowledge and competence (Rhodes 2009). The researchers were able to peruse the completed projects as indirect data for how social interaction might have led to student learning. As interpreters of the phenomena (Lichtman 2013 85), the researchers met weekly to discuss common themes and specific comments made by students that related to the research question. The researchers kept notes of these meetings and individual journals while they reflected on the data.

The survey, guided by the research question, contained open ended items about participants' interactions with other people, their location, and their learning environment while participating in their online course (see Appendix). The instrument was sent to all 33 class participants approximately 5 months after their course was completed, and 10 people responded. Of the respondents, 80% were female and 20% were male. A majority of the respondents were 23 years or younger, revealing that most of the respondents were likely in the study abroad program rather than in the adult learning program. Once all the surveys were collected, the open ended responses were coded with the HyperRESEARCH 3.0 and HyperTRANSCRIBE 1.5.3 softwares. The coding process began with open coding, and as common themes began to emerge from the participant's input, the researchers also looked for the relationships these themes had with each other.

Research Findings

After coding data from the survey results and comparing them with student comments in the course assignments, three major themes were identified as salient to the research question: *flexibility, travel,* and *communication*. Each theme relates to the research question regarding the relationship of past and current experiences with student learning.

Flexibility

Students appreciated the *flexibility* the online course gave them as they attempted to balance studies with traveling abroad or with their adult learning contexts (see Merriam et al., 2007, 66; Sandmann, 2010, 223; Westbrook, 2017, 87). As subthemes of *flexibility*, "time" and "location" shed light on the contexts of the participants and how they understood flexibility. In close connection to "flexible," the descriptor "convenient" surfaced multiple times in the survey responses; however, convenient was used within the context of time. The respondents were able to fit in their studies around travels if they were study abroad students and around employment and taking care of their family's needs if they were adult learners. Convenient did not imply "easy" in the way the participants used the term.

Regarding "time," the students reported that they were able to participate in this online course on their "own time," and the time of day they worked online varied. In addition, the days they worked in the course was driven by their contexts. One study abroad participant wrote, "I would typically do a lot of work on the class in one sitting since we had such an irregular schedule the entire summer.... Sometimes I did everything in the middle of the day, sometimes I did it all in the morning, and sometimes I stayed up past midnight working on it." Those who were not studying abroad and could fit their work into a regular schedule reported set times when they would interact with the online course, for example: "I mainly went to Starbucks a couple nights a week to work on it, usually for a few hours." Another student wrote, "I usually worked on class work in the evenings—usually several hours at a time." Others reported morning as their preferred time to work on the class. One of the adult learners who had to balance work, school, and family reported, "I did a majority of the work at home at night or on the weekends. I worked full time while taking the course." The key feature to this sub-theme of time is that the participants selected the right days and times of day that would give them the opportunity to engage in learning. The *flexibility* of the online course granted empowerment of their learning experiences. *Flexibility* in this sense of empowerment supports Carver et al.'s (2007) use of agency and Westbrook's (2015) report of "time as commodity" as important values for successful online learning.

Second, the *flexibility* of the online course gave students the choice of where they could study. Locations varied from working at home, the library, on campus, and in coffee shops. Their choice of location was sometimes pragmatic in that they logged into the course where they could get the most reliable Wifi connection. One person wrote, "So on days that we were not traveling … I would get a cup of tea, sit in a relatively quieter [*sic.*] room at the villa, and do up to 3 modules in a day." Another student mentioned the "kitchen table" as her or his preferred place to work online. As noted above, "Starbucks" was specifically mentioned as a location of choice. Although this survey did not approach learning styles and preferences, it is difficult to overlook the educational implications of how students may gravitate toward their learning styles when they get to choose where they learn and how they learn.

The theme *flexibility* indirectly relates to the research question of this study. Given that the research question focuses primarily on past and current experiences of the students, their reports of when and where they participated suggest a context in which their current experiences would take place. Indeed, the hours of reading and writing at the kitchen table, in a coffee shop, or in a study room are experiences that contributed to the learning situation.

Travel

Travel was the second major theme that surfaced from the data analysis. This theme applies directly to the research question of how past and current experiences relate to one's learning situation. Two student learning outcomes for the selected course speak to the international scope of this course: "develop solutions for sharing the message of Christ domestically, interculturally, and internationally" and "evaluate the place of intercultural studies, missions strategies, world religious dialog, and the history of missions in world-wide evangelism." Given the global Christian evangelistic nature of the course, one should not be surprised that participants' travel experiences, both past and present, would contribute to the their learning. Bennett (2008) describes the benefit of intercultural experiences for learning in this way: "By combining the interdisciplinary perspectives offered in intercultural communication, international studies, language, and education, an effective approach to intercultural learning readily emerges" (22).

As the participants reflected on their past experiences, several mentioned mission trips or other traveling that related to how they processed the course content. Even high school aged mission trips or overseas experiences left impressions that would help students in this online course. In answer to the survey question "In what ways have your previous life experiences influenced your thinking about world Christianity?," one student responded, "My church back in Arizona did mission trips around the States, and whenever I got the opportunity to go I would…. Going to places of poverty *really made me think* [emphasis added] and realize … that I could help them." Another person shared, "I have been on three mission trips to Mexico with the church I have grown up in, and that definitely gave me a passion for spreading the gospel." In addition, a student noted, "I've been on mission trips before so that helped *shape my understanding* [emphasis added] of cross-cultural experiences." Although church trips were the most often cited experience, any intercultural experience provided backgrounds as possible resources for learning, for example: "I also travel[ed] to Greece and Israel for two weeks with Scholars Abroad where *my eyes were opened* [emphasis added] to new and … different cultures from anything I previously experienced." Not only do these statements demonstrate the lingering impact short international trips can make, but the statements also show evidence of past experiences as a means for processing new learning.

In contrast to previous life experiences as resources, two people indicated that they did not know much about "world Christianity" prior to taking the online course. One person mentioned how he or she had studied other religions and denominations before but "enjoyed delving deeper into those" through the online class. This bit of feedback finds its place on the Dewey learning situation in that the course became the experience that led to learning new content.

While not everyone thought that their geographical location had any bearing on their learning, some did: "I was in Florence, Italy, and this class factored into my learning experience by helping me to keep what is truly important in perspective.... It helped me to remember and more fully understand that everyone in the world ... is an unconditionally and immensely loved child of God who needs Him alone." This student's statement corresponds to another syllabus listed student learning outcome: "develop a compassionate, Christological response to individuals or groups who do not know Christ." One of the adult learners located in the same state as the main campus wrote, "There is a lot of diversity in this city, thus it really opened my eyes to the needs of the people in my community in regard to hearing about Jesus."

Those who participated online from the main campus reported minimal impact of their location on their learning. The data do not indicate why students who were on the main campus did not think that their location had any impact on their learning, but one could infer that the mundane routine of being in a familiar area sparked less attention toward cultural differences than those who were in new and different places.

Communication

Communication was the third major theme of this study. In both the course assignments and survey, participants addressed the importance of communication in their learning experience. Particularly, the participants mentioned the communication with the course facilitator, interaction in the online discussion threads, and face-to-face conversations with others not in the course.

The survey asked students to describe things they did not like about previous online courses. An overwhelming majority complained about the lack of interaction with their professors. It seems that the degree of participation from their professors made an impact on the overall learning within their courses. One student wrote, "I also did not like that I felt such a disconnection from the teacher.... I had basically no contact with the professor.... I just generally like to have a knowledge of what the teacher looks like and know a little bit about their personality." Other comments in the survey had similar criticisms: "[online] hinders the communication between the student and the professor in some cases"; "every class is set up differently so it can be hard to navigate if the teacher doesn't give adequate instructions"; and "no face-to-face conversation." Given that the survey did not ask the participants specifically about the course facilitation, there were no direct comments about the level of the professor's participation in this study. The negative comments they made were about previous online experiences, but they reveal how lack of communication might be associated with poor learning environments. These comments echo Carver et al. (2007) and their concept of belongingness as an important attribute to experiential online learning.

When asked about conversations with people in the online course of this study, several positive evaluations were made by the participants. One person reported that the discussions provided "new insights" than what would have been attained "just by the book alone." Other comments expressed appreciation for the student-to-student interactions: "I really liked seeing other people's opinion in the discussion groups"; "it helped me to see different points of view"; and "I enjoyed reading the different perspectives from all different kinds of people." Furthermore, participants drew a connection between their learning and their online discussions: "the conversations on the discussion boards in the class definitely helped my learning in the class" and "[I] learned lots from others." In contrast to previous experiences in which lack of communication resulted in frustration, the good communication with fellow classmates led to self-reported learning.

Participants were also asked to share how conversations with people outside of the class influenced their learning. Such conversations would have included interviews with people of other cultures and other people with whom participants would have been encouraged to visit about course content. According to one student, "[Conversations outside of class] gave many new insights to the questions that were being asked that allowed me to gain even more insight than I would have by just the book alone." Another student wrote, "My conversations with the Italians who worked at the villa influenced my learning in the class mostly because I got to hear about some of their experiences with faith, which were so different than my experiences." One participant reported how the course affected how the student interacted with others outside of class: "I would say that my learning in [this course] influenced my conversations with others more than the other way around." Consider in the following statement how discussions with parents helped clarify the student's thinking: "Oftentimes if I got stuck or if something really stuck with me, I would talk to my parents about it. They really helped me talk through some things."

In addition to the survey responses, the researchers also reviewed comments in the discussion boards that pointed toward the *communication* theme as valuable for learning. In two assignments, students were asked to interview people outside of the class and report their experiences in the threaded discussion. One student wrote, "I learned a good little snippet from this exercise." Another indicated that reading a classmate's post reminded her of the interview she conducted. A third student commended a classmate for interviewing his own father, writing, "Our parents are our first teachers, and we learn a lot from them." While reflecting on the benefit of learning Greek culture from a Greek person, a student reported: "It was so beneficial for me to get to talk to [a Greek individual] today and to get to learn about Greece as I study here." Overall, there was appreciation and educational value associated to the students' time with other people outside of class.

The theme *communication* connects directly to the research question in that the reports of discussions with classmates and those outside of class helped the students understand course materials better. In terms of the Dewey learning situation, their current experiences with others helped the learners process new ideas and lead to educative moments.

Summary of Findings

The survey surfaced three salient themes: *flexibility, travel,* and *communication.* Each theme was reported to contribute to student learning. *Flexibility* was understood in terms of time and location. Participants appreciated the convenience of being able to contribute to online work on their "own time" and in locations that suited their learning preferences and contextual demands, whether they were students in travel abroad programs with limited Internet connection or adult learners who had to schedule their online interaction around jobs, parenting, and other personal responsibilities. *Travel* reflected directly the research question's concern of the impact of past and current experiences on learning. Both past travels and current study abroad programs provided useful experiences that generated mental frameworks for assimilating new knowledge from their online course experiences. *Communication* also connected to the research question's interest in the impact of experience in that students benefited from online dialog with classmates as well as conversations pertaining to course principles with individuals outside of class, in particular, with people of other cultures that led to understanding anthropological principles.

In the Name of Education

Over twenty years ago Dede (1996) acknowledged pedagogical challenges distance educators face when he distinguished between "knowledge webs," "virtual communities," "synthetic environments," and "sensory immersion" models of distance education. The knowledge web model simply provides content for students to learn or access. Virtual communities imitate face-to-face conversations through online interaction. Synthetic environments simulate real-life situations, such as a flight simulator for student pilots. Sensory immersion uses technology to create the "illusion" of sensory experiences. While Dede anticipated the day when "sensory immersion might ... be combined with knowledge webs, virtual collaboration, and synthetic environments to enable powerful forms of distributed learning" (1996, 28), he also noted how new forms of distance education would not replace valuable face-to-face human interaction. He correctly concluded: "The most significant influence on the evolution of distance education will not be the technical development of more powerful devices but the professional development of wise designers, educators, and learners" (Dede, 1996, 30).

As Cassady and Mullen (2006) have shown, EFTs can provide students vivid and powerful imagery useful for learning. Their experiment also included social interaction between students and facilitators. However, online interaction alone ignores valuable resources students encounter each day. Savicki's (2008) book records the value of face-to-face experiences in study abroad programs. Lowe and Lowe's (2010) application of Bronfenbrenner's (1979) ecology of development to distance education bridges the virtual with the actual by emphasizing one's context as a resource for learning. Finally, Garrison and Vaughan's (2008) community of inquiry applied to blended learning demonstrates how distance education can be seen more broadly than merely web-based social connectedness. Not all distance learning programs may be offered in a blended model, but unless students are in confined isolation, students who learn at a distance may invite people in their contexts into dialog, thus creating a localized version of a community of inquiry. The participants of this study support the literature by demonstrating that past and current experiences as well as interaction with others creates a personalized learning space conducive to achieving student learning outcomes in an online course.

This brief revisit to Dewey's emphasis of educative experiences reinforces to online course designers how significantly their designs contribute to the growth of the students. In addition to an emphasis on content, course designers are to create learning environments that motivate students, challenge them, and maximize their natural tendencies for learning. While digitally produced sensory stimuli may imitate face-to-face encounters with people, places, or events, an online presence need not replace the in-person interactions with friends, family, and colleagues who might be willing to enter into their thought world. The key to quality distance education is not more technology, although technology will continue to improve, but rather the blending of the best technology with the best of in-person interaction in order to achieve student learning outcomes. Listed here are a few possible ways to generate more in-person sensory experiences within online learning environments:

- *Informal conversations.* Facilitators require students to interact with colleagues, peers, or family, allowing the social interaction to be personally relevant.
- *Service learning.* Students engage in service learning projects, such as tutoring children or working in a non-profit organization. Many disciplines would have applications in such settings.
- *Interviews.* Have students interview people in their community and report their conversations to the class online.
- *Field trips.* Facilitators assign real, personalized field trips. Many communities have a nearby museum, park, or relevant institution or organization that provide invaluable opportunities to interact and learn from people and places close to home.

- *Guided conversations.* Students converse with members of their family or social circles following a list of exploratory prompts that connect course content to real world issues.
- *Summative assessments.* Teachers assign summative assessments that require students to contextualize their learning into a useful tool in their own setting.

These are only a few suggestions, but they illustrate how online courses can have meaningful assignments that create genuine learning experiences in the students' contexts. Dewey's principles of experience invite course designers and distance education administrators to move beyond the digital box and to create designs that tap into resources for creating educative experiences for the students, no matter what the media for information transmission might be.

References

Baasanjav, U. (2013). Incorporating the experiential learning cycle into online classes. *MERLOT Journal of Online Learning and Teaching, 9*(4), 575-589.

Bartley, J. (2006). Assessment is as assessment does: A conceptual framework for understanding online assessment and measurement. In M. Hricko and S. L. Howell (Eds.), *Online assessment and measurement: Foundations and challenges* (pp. 1-45). Hershey, PA: Information Science Publishing.

Bennett, J. (2008). On becoming a global soul: A path to engagement during study abroad. In V. Savicki (Ed.), *Developing intercultural competence and transformation: Theory, research, and application in international education* (pp. 1-10). Sterling, Virginia: Stylus.

Bronfenbrenner, U. (1979). *The ecology of human development.* Cambridge, MA: Harvard University Press.

Bruce, B. C., and Levin, J. A. (1997). Educational technology: Media for inquiry, communication, construction, and expression. *Journal of Educational Computing Research, 17*(1), 79-102.

Carver, R., King, R., Hannum, W., and Fowler, B. (2007). Toward a model of experiential e-learning. *MERLOT Journal of Online Learning and Teaching, 3*(3), 247-256.

Cassady, J. C., and Mullen, L. J. (2006). Reconceptualizing electronic field trips: A Deweyian perspective. *Learning, Media and Technology, 31*(2), 149-161.

Collins, A., and Halverson, R. (2009). *Rethinking education in the age of technology: The digital revolution and school in America.* New York: Teachers College Press.

Conrad, R.-M., and Donaldson, J. A. (2004). *Engaging the online learner: Activities and resources for creative instruction.* San Francisco: Jossey-Bass.

Cremin, L. A. (1961). *The transformation of the school: Progressivism in American education, 1876-1957.* New York: Knopf.

Dede, C. (1996). Distance learning—distributed learning: Making the transformation. *Learning and Leading with Technology, 23*(7), 25-30.

Dewey, J. (1900). *The school and society.* Chicago: The University of Chicago Press.

_____. (1916). *Democracy and education: An introduction to the philosophy of education.* N.p.

_____. (1938). *Experience and education.* New York: Touchstone.

Dewey, J. (2005). *How we think*. The Barnes and Noble Library of Essential Reading. New York: Barnes and Noble.

Eames, S. M. (1977). *Pragmatic naturalism: An introduction*. Carbondale, IL: Southern Illinois University Press.

Froebel, F. (1906). *The education of man*. (W. N. Hailmann, Trans.). New York: D. Appleton.

Gall, M. D., Gall, J. P., and Borg, W. R. (2007). *Education research: An introduction*. Boston: Pearson.

Gamson, D. A. (2003). District progressivism: Rethinking reform in urban school systems, 1900-1928. *Paedagogica Historica, 39*(4), 417-34.

Garrison, R. D., and Vaughan, N. D. (2008). *Blended learning in higher education: Framework, principles, and guidelines*. San Francisco: Jossey-Bass.

Graham, C. R. (2006). Blended learning systems: Definition, current trends, and future directions. In C. J. Bonk and C. R. Graham (Eds.), *The handbook of blended learning: Global perspectives, local designs* (3-21). San Francisco: Pfeiffer.

Hawkes, M., and Romiszowski, A. (2001). Examining the reflective outcomes of asynchronous computer-mediated communication on inservice teacher development. *Journal of Technology and Teacher Education, 9*(2), 285-308.

Howell, G. S., Lacour, M. M., and McGlawn, A. (2017). Construction student knowledge in the online classroom: The effectiveness of focal prompts. *College Student Journal, 51*(4), 483.

Kolb, D. A. (1984). *Experiential learning: Experience as the source of learning and development*. Upper Saddle River, NJ: Prentice Hall.

Koontz, F. R., Li, H., and Compora, D. (2006). *Designing effective online instruction: A handbook for web-based courses.* Lanham, MD: Rowman and Littlefield Education.

Legon, R. and Garrett, R. (2017). *The changing landscape of online education (CHLOE): Quality Matters and Eduventures survey of chief online officers.* Annapolis: Quality Matters and Eduventures.

Lichtman, M. (2013). *Qualitative research in education: A user's guide.* Los Angeles: Sage.

Lou, K. H., and Bosley, G. W. (2008). Dynamics of cultural contexts: Meta-level intervention in the study abroad experience. In V. Savicki (Ed.), *Developing intercultural competence and transformation: Theory, research, and application in international education* (276-296). Sterling, Virginia: Stylus.

Lowe, S. D., and Lowe, M. E. (2010). Spiritual formation in theological distance education: An ecosystems model. *Christian Education Journal,* 3, 7(1), 85-102.

Mason, R., and Rennie, F. (2008). *E-learning and social networking handbook: Resources for higher education.* New York: Routledge.

Merriam, S. (2009). *Qualitative research: A guide to design and implementation.* San Francisco: Jossey-Bass.

Merriam, S., Caffarella, R., and Baumgartner, L. (2007). *Learning in adulthood: A comprehensive guide.* San Francisco: Jossey-Bass.

Noddings, N. (2012). *Philosophy of education* (3rd ed.). Boulder, CO: Westview Press.

Patton, M. Q. (2002). *Qualitative research and evaluation methods.* Thousand Oaks: Sage.

Reese, W. J. (2001). The origins of progressive education. *History of Education Quarterly,* 40(Spring), vi-24.

Rhodes, T. (2009). *Assessing outcomes and improving achievement: Tips and tools for using the rubrics.* Washington, DC: Association of American Colleges and Universities.

Rice, J. M. (1893). *The public-school system of the United States.* New York: The Century Company.

Roberts, J. (2007). Education, eco-progressivism and the nature of school reform. *Educational Studies, 41*(3), 212-229.

Rousseau, J.-J. (1979). *Emile or on education.* (A. Bloom, Trans.). New York: Basic Books.

Sandmann, L. (2010). Adults in four-year colleges and universities: Moving from the margin to mainstream? In C. E. Kasworm, A.D. Rose, and J. M. Ross-Gordon, (Eds.), *Handbook of adult and continuing education* (221-230). Los Angeles: Sage.

Savicki, V. (2008). Experiential and affective education for international educators. In V. Savicki (Ed.), *Developing intercultural competence and transformation: Theory, research, and application in international education* (74-91). Sterling, Virginia: Stylus.

Selby, R. (2008). Designing transformation in international education. In V. Savicki (Ed.), *Developing intercultural competence and transformation: Theory, research, and application in international education* (1-10). Sterling, Virginia: Stylus.

Shapiro, M. S. (1983). *Child's garden: The Kindergarten Movement from Froebel to Dewey.* University Park, PA: The Pennsylvania State University Press.

Thor, D. D., Nan, X., Meixun, Z., Ruidan, M., and Xiao Xi, Y. (2017). An interactive online approach to small-group student presentations and discussions. *Advances in Physiology Education, 41*(4), 498-504.

Volk, K. S. (2005). The Gary Plan and technology education: What might have been? *The Journal of Technology Studies, 31*(Winter), 39-48.

Wagner, E. D. (2006). On designing interaction experiences for the next generation of blended learning. In C. J. Bonk and C. R. Graham (Eds.), *The handbook of blended learning: Global perspectives, local designs* (41-59). San Francisco: Pfeiffer.

Wallace, J. M. (2006). Chapter Six: Preserving progressivism in a junior high school: PS 45, 1929-1944. In J. M. Wallace (Ed.), *The promise of progressivism: Angelo Patri and urban education* (79-98). New York: Peter Lang Publishing.

Westbrook, T. (2015). Embracing the mission: A case study of adjunct faculty perceptions of online problem-based learning for professional development. *An eJournal of Faith-Based Learning, 1*(1), 1-26.

_____. (2017). *Spirituality, community, and race consciousness in adult higher education: Breaking the cycle of racialization.* New York, NY: Routledge.

Appendix

Survey for [name of the online class]

This survey asks you about your experiences in your online [name of the online class] at [name of the university]. Thank you for taking time to answer these survey questions.

Your participation in this research survey is voluntary, and if you choose to fill out the form, you may withdraw at any time or leave any items blank without any repercussions. Furthermore, your participation is strictly confidential. As the research is shared professional and public audiences, no one will be able to identify your comments as your own. You will be protected in this way. Finally, this research is being conducted in compliance with and approval of the Institutional Research Board at [name of the university].

Demographic and Introductory Information

What is your gender?

What is your age?

What is your race?

What is your marital status?

What is your classification?

What is your major or degree program?

Do you have a job? If so, what is it?

Where did you attend high school? Was it public, private, or homeschool? Or a combination?

If you attended a college besides [name of the university], where did you go?

Experiences in [name of the online class]

Describe the things you liked about online classes you have taken prior to [name of the class] online.

Describe the things you didn't like about online classes you have taken prior to [name of the class] online.

Describe your typical setting for participating in this online class? Where did you work? What time of day? How much time did it take?

In what ways have your previous life experiences influenced your thinking about world Christianity?

What other activities or classes, if any, were you involved in while taking [name of the online class]?

In what ways did your conversations with other people outside of class influence your learning in [name of the online class]?

In what ways did your conversations with people in the class influence your learning in [name of the online class]?

In which city were you when you took [name of the class] online; and in what ways, if any, did this location factor into your learning experience?

5

Teaching Presence (Course Design, Direct Instruction, and Facilitated Discourse) and the Impact on Student Success in Online Learning

Victoria Dunnam

Introduction

What is "Teaching Presence," and why is it important? In order for students to succeed academically, the Community of Inquiry (COI) model suggests that three elements must be present: teaching presence, social presence and cognitive presence (Garrison, 2007; Garrison, 2011; Garrison and Akyol, 2015; Garrison et al., 2000; Giannousi and Kioumourtzoglou, 2016; Rockinson-Szapkiw, Wendt, Wighting, and Nisbet, 2016; Shea and Bidjerano, 2013). Many studies have been conducted using the COI model using self-reported instruments (Garrison et al., 2000; Garrison, 2007; Shea and Bidjerano, 2013). These studies have included a focus on student success (Rockinson-Szapkiw et al., 2016), student satisfaction (Giannousi and Kioumourtzoglou, 2016; Miller, Hahs-

Vaughn, and Zygouris-Coe, 2014), student perceptions of learning (Hosler and Arend, 2012), motivation (Baker and Taylor, 2012; Kim and Frick, 2011), and learning styles (Mouzouri, 2016) in regards to the COI model. Literature review shows research studies used self-report instruments and others have used data mining or learning analytics to examine student interactions in online courses. I use learning analytics for my own study.

There is a shift in examining and analyzing learning performance in online learning. For over a decade, learning management systems have been storing data of every student click during an online course, but institutions have not utilized analyzing this data to gain insight on student learning patterns. Gathering data from the learning management system to measure and analyze students' actions to gain a better understanding of the learning experience is part of this shift. One way to analyze student's performance in online learning is using learning analytics, which allows students usage data stored in the learning management system to be extracted and analyzed. The data benefit instructors as they create online courses, instructional designers who help develop course content, and administrators who would benefit from the analysis of this data. This type of analysis helps educators make decisions to improve student learning in online courses (Romero, Ventura, and García, 2008).

Designing online courses that incorporate instructional strategies that promote student learning is one of the challenges that still exists among educators. There seems to be a lack of consensus on which instructional strategies are most effective in integrating teaching presence when developing a sense of community among learners (Corrin et al., 2016; Phirangee, Epp, and Hewitt, 2016). This lack of consensus regarding instructional strategies could be due in part to the lack of reliable analytics that can provide detailed information on how the students interact with components within the online course. To evaluate the effectiveness of teaching and learning, learning analytics can provide a powerful resource for researchers and teachers (Corrin et al., 2016). Learning analytics can provide the means to explain students' online behaviors and help meet this challenge of designing online courses that incorporate instructional strategies to improve student learning.

What Is Teaching Presence?

Teaching presence as defined by Garrison et al. (2000; Garrison, 2007; Shea and Bidjerano, 2013) consists of three key elements: course design, direct instruction and facilitated discourse. Teaching presence is vital to student learning. The effective instructional design incorporates these three elements when producing online courses, guiding the learning process, and is established through student-content interactions (Gašević et al., 2015a; Lim, 2007). Baker and Taylor (2012), confirmed that teaching presence is essential to successful student learning. Students benefit from courses that are designed to promote a positive learning environment and from instructors who commu-nicate with students in order to motivate them to be successful in the course and to personalize the learning experience. Teaching presence in online courses corresponds to how the instructor designs the course, facilitates communication, and develops course content and learning activities. There are different means of performing teaching presence in online courses that can bring different effective levels of teaching presence (Zhao and Sullivan, 2017).

Course design describes the instructor's role in developing and managing the course and is known as student-system interactions (Zhao and Sullivan, 2017). Research has noted that student-system (also known as student-interface) interactions are important in online learning. This interaction is the student's interaction with the use of electronic tools and navigating within the course. Romero et al. (2013) stated the importance of students being familiar with unique features of the interface, which, increased not only interaction with the interface, but also interaction with others in the online course.

Direct instruction is based on the instructor's function as a content facilitator as one uses resources to deliver content to the students (Chen, 2001; Nandi et al., 2015). The constructivist view of the COI model holds that teaching presence is established through student-to-content interactions (Lim, 2007). Teaching presence through direct instruction is the means where students interact with course instructional materials (Agudo-Peregrina et al., 2014; Swan et al., 2008). Student-content interactions happen when "students make use of content resources such as textbooks, documents, research materials, videos, audios or other learning materials" (Agudo-Peregrina et al., 2014, 544). When students click on resources in a course such as web pages, lectures, and instructional documents, the action reflects the teaching presence element in direct instruction.

When students interact with instructors by sharing meaning from information provided by instructional materials, the student to instructor interaction is known as "facilitating discourse" (Gašević et al., 2015a; Lim, 2007; Swan et al., 2008). The definition of student-instructor interactions is also known as "dialogue between students and the instructor" (Abrami, Bernard, Bures, Borokhovski, and Tamim, 2012, 86). Examples of student-instructor interactions include direct messaging or discussion forums (Agudo-Peregrina et al., 2014; Al Ghamdi et al., 2016). Facilitated discourse fosters student-centered approaches in discussions and feedback within the online course (Chen, 2001; Nandi et al., 2015; Zhao and Sullivan, 2017). When students interact with the instructor, and the instructor interacts with students via messaging, chats, or discussion forums, the discourse allows the researcher to examine teaching presence in facilitated discourse.

Course Design

Course design describes the instructor's role in designing and managing the course (Arbaugh, 2014; Zhao and Sullivan, 2017). Teaching presence begins before the course starts when the instructor is designing and planning the course and continues during the course as the instructor directs instruction and facilitates discourse (Zhao and Sullivan, 2017). The instructor plays a significant role in the course design. Each feature of the course design serves a purpose and allows the student to interact with the unique features to promote learning and communication. In online learning, it is important for students to have self-efficacy in navigating through various components of the course design.

Researchers have found it important for the student to be familiar with navigating a course and having the ability to interact with technological tools as crucial and necessary to the learning process (Romero et al., 2013). Romero et al. (2013) stated the importance of students being familiar with unique features of the interface, which increased not only interaction with the interface, but also interaction with others in the online course. Instructors who have clear learning outcomes support students' efforts to navigate the course and to make meaning from the course content. Hosler and Arend (2012) study confirmed that students felt the design and organization of the course helped keep the student focused. Ramos and Yudko (2008) stated that "positive learner-interface interaction impacts all other forms of online communication and the overall course experience" (p.1175).

Learning begins as soon as a student opens a course. The student must learn to navigate the course and find the relevant content, assignments, quizzes, and discussions. This aspect of learning begins before the student accesses any materials or posts any assignments or discussions. One cannot dismiss the importance of a well-designed course because this phase of learning provides the foundation for future learning. For this reason, it is important to examine how the student interacts with course features to provide a lens to examine how well a student succeeds in an online course (Alsadhan et al., 2014). When students click on the course schedule, course calendar, or navigate to course overview tutorials, they are using examples of teaching presence course design features. Examining how many times students interact with the course design features allows the researcher to identify patterns and behaviors for teaching presence in course design.

Course design is represented as student-system interactions. Teaching presence through direct instruction is based on the instructors' function as a content facilitator as they use resources to deliver content to the students and is represented as student-content interactions. Teaching presence through facilitated discourse fosters learner-centered approaches in discussions, and feedback within the online course (Zhao and Sullivan, 2017). Teaching presence facilitated discourse is represented as student-instructor interactions. Teaching presence relates to how the student interacts with the instructor, instructional tools, and learning activities. Students' interactions with course content are represented as student-content interactions. Students' interactions with instructors are represented as student-instructor interactions.

Direct Instruction

Direct instruction is an element of the COI model teaching presence. Direct instruction is based on the instructor's function as a content facilitator as one uses resources to deliver content to the students (Zhao and Sullivan, 2017). Direct instruction occurs when instructors are engaged in presenting course content through resources and other course content activities (Lynch, 2016). The instructor provides feedback and determines students' understanding of the course content. Students may access the course content any time during the duration of the course. It is important to note that interactions between the instructor and student do not require synchronous communication.

Instructors post instructions, lectures, and pages that are examples of asynchronous instructor-to-student interaction. These resources reflect direct instructional materials, lectures, and other resources faculty use to communicate to their students.

This direct instruction provides the method for students to access course materials and learn the content presented. Direct instruction is necessary and occurs before students communicate through discussion forums. Students must learn the material and provide critical thinking before accessing discussion forums to communicate with the instructor and other students about the learning material content.

Previous studies have examined teaching presence and revealed the importance in the learning process (Baker, 2010; Joksimović et al., 2015). There are many methods that define an instructor's presence in an online course. Instructors share information with students through the course materials, lecture videos, through directing students to pertinent websites, and by participating in discussion forums. Students' involvement in discussions is influenced by instructor presence and the quality of student participation, which is beneficial to provide in a learning environment that promotes interaction with one another (Oztok et al., 2013). Studies have shown the importance of instructor presence that contributes to the positive online environment (Arbaugh, 2014). The key to student satisfaction is the instructor's social presence (Ley and Gannon-Cook, 2014). The number of interactions, instructor's presence, and feedback was reported as important (Ma et al., 2015).

Facilitated Discourse

Communication within online learning environments is important to learning and to helping the student feel connected. Baker (2010) stated that instructor presence has statistically significant relation to students' learning, cognition, and motivation. Facilitated discourse fosters learner-centered approaches in discussions and feedback within the online course (Zhao and Sullivan, 2017). The more communication and dialogue between instructors and students, the less students feel disconnected due to geographical distance in online courses (Baker, 2010). The use of electronic communication tools such as discussions, email, chat, and messaging provides methods to increase interactions among instructors and students and reduces the psychological and physical distance (Baker, 2010). Similarly, Hosler and Arend (2012) confirmed that students felt the direct feedback and facilitated discussions in the course helped keep them focused and participating. Facilitating discourse is the ability to encourage student participation by providing feedback and acknowledging students' contributions. Student responses reported in a study conducted by Hosler and Arend (2012) confirmed the need for instructors to provide both group feedback, and individual feedback and that it was important to improving their critical thinking and improving their learning.

Instructor facilitation provides support and guidance in online courses. Phirangee et al. (2016) confirmed students (N=110) from a public research university in Canada prefer instructors to be involved in online discussions, and they needed instructor feedback. The students felt the instructors were subject matter experts and better in guiding the learning than their peers. The findings of Phirangee et al. (2016) support previous research regarding a strong correlation between teaching presence and learning.

Methodology or Methods

My own research examined student interactions (teaching presence elements, course design, direct instruction, and facilitated discourse) and student achievement. The research gathered data from a faith-based university located in the southwestern part of the United States. The study examined the correlation between the teaching presence elements (course design, direct instruction, and facilitated discourse) and social presence and examined if these variables affected student achievement (Dunnam, 2018).

The research examined the following questions:

RQ1: When using learning analytics, is there a significant correlation between the number of student-content interactions and the number of student-student interactions in graduate students taking online courses?

RQ2: When using learning analytics, is there a significant correlation between number of student-instructor interactions and number of student-student interactions in graduate students taking online courses?

RQ3: When using learning analytics, is there a significant correlation between number of student-system inter-actions and number of student-student interactions in graduate students taking online courses?

RQ4: When using learning analytics, does number of student-content interactions, number of student-instruc-tor interactions, number of student-student interactions, and number of student-system interactions predict final student grade as explored with regression analysis in graduate students taking online courses?

As additional analysis, I examined if the individual variable (course design, direct instruction, or facilitated discourse) were predictive of student final grade.

Results of Study

The results for research question one showed student-content interaction (teaching presence: direct instruction) had a medium-to-large strongly positive and statistically significant correlation to student-student (social presence). This signifies the importance of instructional content to learning in an online course.

The results for research question two showed student-instructor (teaching presence: facilitated discourse) had a medium, strongly positive and statistically significant correlation to student-student (social presence). This signifies the importance of instructor presence to learning in an online course.

The results for research question three showed student-system (teaching presence: course design) had a strongly positive and statistically significant correlation to student-student (social presence). Romero et al. (2013) demonstrated the importance of students being familiar with unique features of the course. Those results suggest that this familiarity increased not only interaction with the interface, but also interaction with others in the online course.

The results for research question four examined if all student interactions (student-content, student-instructor, student-student, and student-system) were predictive of student final course grade. The results showed that all the variables together were not predictive of student final grade. However, additional analysis examined each variable separately to see if the variable was predictive of student final grade. The results showed that student-instructor (teaching presence: facilitated discourse) was a significant predictor of grades. It also showed that student-content (teaching presence: direct instruction) was a significant predictor of grades and also student-system (teaching presence: course design) was a predictor of grades. The most interesting part of this additional analysis was the student-system (teaching presence: course design) had the greatest significant predictor of grades. Also, interestingly, student-student (social presence) was not a predictor of grades. Therefore, direct instruction, facilitated discourse and course design were statistically significant in predicting grades (Dunnam, 2018).

Guidelines for Course Design

Instructional designers benefit by evaluating students' click-by-click actions within a course which aids in the course design process, keep an eye on student motivation and how to improve teaching presence. Course design is necessary to increase student motivation, self-regulated learning, and student-student interactions (Bernard et al., 2014; Kim and Frick, 2011). Wright et al. (2014) stated that learning analytics give instructors data analyses of students' actions within the course to help identify student learning needs and to personalize the instruction appropriately.

Course design is important to student success or lack of success in online courses. When a course lacks a clear and purposeful design, then it creates an environment of confusion and frustration on the part of the student. This can definitely affect the student's motivation. Without a clear and definitive easy-to-follow course design may result in students' spending way too much time trying to figure out what to do in the course or where to find the materials they need in the course. Without the proper guidance and course design, the instructor then will spend too much time answering questions and explaining and clarifying expectations to the students instead of spending quality time with meaningful instruction and feedback. When developing an online course, it is crucial to create clear and measurable learning outcomes to help guide the students. Providing structure establishes teaching presence in an online course.

It is important to recognize how the content is organized in the course and how clear the instructions and communication is in your course. When a course is well-designed, it gives opportunities for the instructor to provide meaningful feedback to the students. This feedback provides for a rich communication between instructor and student and provides opportunities for students to feel connected to their instructor. This connection between the instructor and student allows the student to experience the freedom to question and communicate freely with a student to instructor dialogue.

This communication sets the tone for the entire time in the course. Instructors should create written material in a way that is engaging, encouraging, and inviting. This creates a positive learning environment, which encourages students to stay on task and to be motivated to continue learning in the course. The instructor must provide activities that promote ways for an online teaching presence. This online teaching presence does require more preparation time than in a face-to-face classroom. This preparation time should be more "explicit and transparent in design and organization because it differs from face-to-face because the normal social cues are not available" (Kupczynski, Ice, Wiesenmayer, and McCluskey, 2010).

It is important for the instructor to be more explicit and transparent in design and organization because the traditional social cues and norms of the face-to-face classroom are unavailable (Coppola, Hiltz, and Rotter, 2002). Research by Kupczynski, Ice, Wiesenmayer, and McCluskey (2010), indicated that students lack of success was due to instructional design and organization followed by direct instruction and then by facilitation of discourse.

This represents how a poorly constructed course design results in student failure in an online course. On the other hand, the students perceived that items that helped them succeed in an online course was facilitation of discourse, direct instruction, and course design. The study also revealed that student perceived instructor feedback helped them understand their strengths and weaknesses. It was important for instructors to be transparent about their thinking on a topic and as well as model how to use that information in the course and later. Students perceived the lack of feedback as part of their failure in a course.

In course design when instructors inadequately provide clear instruction on a course topic or provide clear instructions on how the student can participate in course activities, they are making it difficult for students to be successful in their course. From an instructional design perspective, the need for presentation of "clear, concise objectives, instructions and general participation guidelines should be cornerstone of online course development" (Kupczynski, Ice, Wiesenmayer, and McCluskey, 2010, 32).

Below are some guidelines for providing teaching presence (course design, direct instruction, and facilitated discourse) in online courses:

Course Design Guidelines:

1. Importance of consistent course design
   Design should include the type of font used, the size of the font, placement of videos or images. Remember that larger font usually means that section of text is

more important than other tests. The use of text boxes can convey that information as well. Making your course visually attractive helps establish these guidelines and importance in the course. Consistent course design is very important when creating a program within multiple courses so that the design for the course is consistent throughout all courses in that program.

2. Make sure that each section such as module or week has stated the course and module learning objectives. This information helps students know what they will be learning and what they will be able to do when completing the week/module in the course.

3. The navigation within the course should be well organized, logical, consistent, and efficient. Students should not have to hunt for information. The course design should be easy to navigate.

4. The instructional content should be clearly explained so students understand the purpose of the content.

5. If using particular engaging technology tools, providing the students with instructions on how to use these tools is very important.

Direct Instruction Guidelines:

1. Create student engagement in active learning activities.

2. Providing a variety of perspectives and multiple formats of the instructional content should be available.

Examples of these variety would be having a video lecture also available in text transcript or available in audio only.

3. Any instructional content should be cited properly.

4. Content given to students should be placed in "chunks" in clearly labeled, organized segments in the course. Chunks of information also known as "scaffolding" which allows student to absorb smaller chunks of information and helps in the learning process.

5. Provide both synchronous and asynchronous activities throughout the course.

6. Provide a variety of options for completing assignments (eg. video or audio response in discussions versus always writing their responses or replies).

7. Locate and use content resources that are available in a digital format if possible.

Facilitated Discourse Guidelines:

1. Introduce yourself to the students at the beginning of the course.

2. Create virtual office hours so students can contact you periodically during the course.

3. Use tools like Remind 101 to send reminders to students or just send a fun fact or a fun picture of something you are doing to make yourself more approachable.

4. Ask for informal feedback from students at beginning of the course.

5. Actively communicate with them in discussion forums.

6. Be timely in posting responses to their questions.

7. Provide feedback comments on their assignments and quizzes in a timely manner.

8. Provide surveys after each week/module to assess the learning materials or problems students may be experiencing instead of waiting until the end of the course.

Conclusion

Teaching presence (course design, direct instruction, and facilitated discourse) plays an important role in students' learning process. The role of the instructor in creating and designing the course, providing instructional course content, and communicated with students encompass the COI Model of teaching presence. This article has given insight on my experience in online learning and in research regarding teaching presence. Course design involves the instructor's role in developing and managing the course. Direct instructor is the instructor's function as a content facilitator as instructors use resources to deliver content to the students. Facilitated discourse is the instructor's role to facilitate and foster learner-centered approaches in discussions and feedback within the course. Each of these elements of teaching presence is crucial to the learning process and providing a positive and quality learning environment for students within online learning courses.

References

Abrami, C., Bernard, R. M., Bures, E. M., Borokhovski, E., and Tamim, R. M. (2012). Interaction in distance education and online learning: Using evidence and theory to improve practice. *The Next Generation of Distance Education* (49-69). Springer US.

Agudo-Peregrina, A. F., Iglesias-Pradas, S., Conde-Gonzalez, M. A., and Hernandez- Garcia, A. (2014). Can we predict success from log data in VLEs? Classification of interactions for learning analytics and their relation with performance in VLE-supported F2F and online learning. *Computers in Human Behavior*, 1, 542-550.

Al Ghamdi, A., Samarji, A., and Watt, A. (2016). Essential considerations in distance education in KSA: Teacher immediacy in a virtual teaching and learning environment. *International Journal of Information and Education Technology*, 6(1), 17.

Alsadhan, A. O., Alhomod, S., and Shatl, M. M. (2014). Multimedia based E-learning: Design and integration of multimedia content in E-learning. *International Journal of Emerging Technologies in Learning*, 9(3), 26-30.

Arbaugh, J. B. (2014). System, scholar or students? Which most influences online MBA course effectiveness? *Journal of Computer Assisted Learning*, 30(4), 349-362.

Baker, R. S. J. D. (2010). Data mining for education. *International Encyclopedia of Education*, 7, 112-118.

Baker, C., and Taylor, S. L. (2012). The importance of teaching presence in an online course. *Online Student Engagement Tools and Strategies*, 5.

Chen, Y. (2001). Dimensions of transactional distance in the world wide web learning environment: A factor analysis. *British Journal of Educational Technology, 32*(4), 459-470.

Coppola, N. W., Hiltz, S. R., and Rotter, N. G. (2002). Becoming a virtual professor: Pedagogical roles and asynchronous learning networks. *Journal of Management Information Systems,* 18(4), 169-189.

Corrin, L., Kennedy, G., de Barba, G., Lockyer, L., Gasevic, D., Williams, D., and Bakharia, A. (2016). Completing the loop: Returning meaningful learning analytic data to teachers. Sydney: Office for Learning and Teaching.

Dunnam, M. V. (2018). Correlational study examining graduate students' online interactions and academic achievement using learning analytics (Doctoral dissertation, Grand Canyon University).

Garrison, D. R. (2007). Online community of inquiry review: Social, cognitive, and teaching presence issues. *Journal of Asynchronous Learning Networks, 11*(1), 61- 72.

Garrison, D. R. (2011). *E-learning in the 21ˢᵗ Century: A frame-work for research and practice,* 2ⁿᵈ Edition. NY: Routledge.

Garrison, D. R., and Akyol, Z. (2015). Toward the development of a metacognition construct for communities of inquiry. *The Internet and Higher Education, 24,* 66–71.

Garrison, D. R., Anderson, T., and Archer, W. (2000). Critical inquiry in a text-based environment: Computer conferencing in higher education. *The Internet and Higher Education*, *2*(2), 87–105.

Gašević, D., Adesope, O., Joksimović, S., and Kovanović, V. (2015a). Externally-facilitated regulation scaffolding and role assignment to develop cognitive presence in asynchronous on-line discussions. *The Internet and Higher Education*, *24*, 53-65.

Giannousi, M., and Kioumourtzoglou, E. (2016). Cognitive, social, and teaching presence as predictors of students' satisfaction in distance learning. *Mediterranean Journal of Social Sciences*, *7*(2 S1), 439.

Hosler, K. A., and Arend, B. D. (2012). The importance of course design, feedback, and facilitation: Student perceptions of the relationship between teaching presence and cognitive presence. *Educational Media International*, *49*(3), 217–229.

Joksimović, S., Gašević, D., Loughin, T. M., Kovanović, V., and Hatala, M. (2015). Learning at distance: Effects of interaction traces on academic achievement. *Computers and Education*, *87*, 204-217.

Kim, K.-J., and Frick, T. W. (2011). Changes in student motivation during online learning. *Journal of Educational Computing Research*, *44*(1), 1–23.

Kupczynski, L.; Ice, P.; Wiesenmayer, R.; and McCluskey, F. (2010). Student perceptions of the relationship between indicators of teaching presence and success in online courses. *Journal of Interactive Online Learning*, 9(1), 23-43.

Ley, K., and Gannon-Cook, R. (2014). Learner-valued interactions:

Research into practice. *Quarterly Review of Distance Education, 15*(1), 23.

Lim, H. L. (2007). Community of inquiry in an online undergraduate information technology course. *Journal of Information Technology Education: Research,* 6, 153-168.

Lynch, J. (2016). *What is teaching presence?* Course Design, Development and Academic research. Pearson Education. Retrieved from http://www.pearsoned.com/wp-content/uploads/Teaching-Presence.pdf

Ma, J., Han, X., Yang, J., and Cheng, J. (2015). Examining the necessary condition for engagement in an online learning environment based on learning analytics approach: The role of the instructor. *The Internet and Higher Education, 24,* 26- 34.

Miller, M. G., Hahs-Vaughn, D. L., and Zygouris-Coe, V. (2014). A confirmatory factor analysis of teaching presence within online professional development. Journal of Asynchronous Learning Networks, 18(1).

Mouzouri, H. (2016). The relationships between students' perceived learning styles and the community of inquiry presences in a graduate online course. *International Journal of Emerging Technologies in Learning, 11*(4), 40-47.

Nandi, D., Hamilton, M., and Harland, J. (2015). What Factors Impact Student-Content Interaction in Fully Online Courses. *International Journal of Modern Education and Computer Science, 7*(7), 28.

Oztok, M., Zingaro, D., Brett, C., and Hewitt, J. (2013). Exploring asynchronous and synchronous tool use in online courses. *Computers and Education, 60*(1), 87-94.

Phirangee, K., Epp, C. D., and Hewitt, J. (2016). Exploring the relationships between facilitation methods, students' sense of community and their online behaviours. *Online Learning*, *20*(2).

Ramos, C., and Yudko, E. (2008). "Hits" (not "discussion posts") predict student success in online courses: a double cross-validation study. *Computers and Education*, *50*(4), 1174-1182.

Rockinson-Szapkiw, A. J., Wendt, J., Wighting, M., and Nisbet, D. (2016). The predictive relationship among the community of inquiry framework, perceived learning and online, and graduate students' course grades in online synchronous and asynchronous courses. *International Review of Research in Open and Distance Learning*, *17*(3), 18.

Romero, C., Ventura, S., and García, E. (2008). Data mining in course management systems: Moodle case study and tutorial. *Computers and Education*, *51*(1), 368-384.

Romero, C., Espejo, G., Zafra, A., Romero, J. R., and Ventura, S. (2013). Web usage mining for predicting final marks of students that use Moodle courses. *Computer Applications in Engineering Education*, *21*(1), 135-146.

Shea, P., and Bidjerano, T. (2013). Understanding distinctions in learning in hybrid, and online environments: an empirical investigation of the community of inquiry framework. *Interactive Learning Environments*, *21*(4), 355–370.

Swan, K., Shea, P., Richardson, J., Ice, P., Garrison, D. R., Cleveland-Innes, M., and Arbaugh, J. B. (2008). Validating a measurement tool of presence in online communities of inquiry. *E-mentor*, *2*(24), 1-12.

Zhao, H., and Sullivan, K. (2017). Teaching presence in computer conferencing learning environments: Effects on interaction, cognition and learning uptake. *British Journal of Educational Technology. Vol 48.* No 2 538-551.

Engaging the Learner

6

Engaging Online Students through Customer Service and Pastoral Care Mentality

Sunday Akin Olukoju

Introduction

The current reality of COVID-19 is a curse to the rigid and a blessing to the flexible and the discerning. In the *Forbes* online magazine, Andrew DePietro (2020) says, "Colleges and universities as well as primary and secondary schools have made an enormous shift toward online and virtual courses," hence this chapter offers some ideas on how to engage online students creatively. As an online instructor of over a decade-long uninterrupted online teaching experience, a personal lesson places a lot of emphasis not only on the atmosphere the instructor must create, but also on the way the instructor demonstrates an inviting, calming, fascinating, stress-free and interesting environment. This chapter also introduces customer service and pastoral care mentality in situating a learning environment that will not only enrich and empower online students, but one that also strikes a balance between rigor and vigor. In an age when attention span is so short based on disruptive social media interruptive flood of information, this chapter also introduces some fun ideas that keep the classroom atmosphere warm, despite the physical and social distance between the various online students on one hand and between online students and their instructor on the other hand. While this essay promises to acknowledge the importance of hard skills in midwifing a successfully efficient and effective online education delivery method, it also identifies some highly important soft skills that are indispensable to the entire business of online classroom delivery option, if it must be as productive as the designers desire. Some pastoral care ideas can help improve the spiritual formation piece that seminary education mandates, and few of them will come up in this chapter.

Background to Online Education

Tom Tanner and Eliza Smith Brown (2015) of the Association of Theological Schools share interesting data showing that:

The most common new delivery systems are distance (online) education and extension education. More than half (145 schools or 53 percent) of all ATS members now offer distance education, as contrasted with less than 10 percent just a decade ago. Of those 145, 125 have approval to offer comprehensive distance education (i.e., more than five courses; see list of approved schools on the ATS website). While distance education enrollments are difficult to count (partly due to recent changes in how those numbers are reported), it appears that the number of online students in ATS schools has increased by as much as 35 percent since 2009 (from around 13,750 to around 18,500). This past fall, about one-fourth of all ATS students were enrolled in at least one online course, whereas a decade ago fewer than one-tenth were (2).

Although the above may have been an unplanned occurrence of circumstance, particularly by those working adults who desire to complete graduate education, the current COVID-19 will most likely accelerate a higher preference for online education. And this will mean more interests in this area of online delivery, especially on student engagement and student satisfaction for many new students who may perceive online education as foreign. While Toro-Troconis, Alexander and Frutos-Perez (2019) conclude that "Online learning was acceptable and convenient to postgraduate students" (171), it is interesting to see their study identify products of hard skills as the "three major themes" that "emerged from the focus group," and these are: "weekly forums and webinars," self-directed learning materials," and "learning design and support" (171). Their inability to find a strong "association between average overall mark in all modules and the level of engagement with self-directed content," as well as "between average overall mark in all modules and the level of engagement in collaborative activities" (171) may be due to the study's focus on "online content" and "collaborative activities" rather than what drives the process and how. This is where the human factor comes in, where the necessity for student engagement will force schools to consider the role of customer service approach in enriching student involvement.

The importance of human factor and soft skills come up here. These could lead to a higher level of student engagement as well as a lower level of student withdrawal as Hutton and Robson's (2019) study shows. The involvement of trained tutors and student buddies positively changed the class interaction and students' engagement dynamics.

It is also imperative to identify some specific expectations that should guide the distance/online philosophy of education. These will form the solid foundation upon which every instructor training should depend in order to get an institution-wide branding that will attract, engage, retain, and help current students to finish successfully and satisfactorily. The outcome of this will also be an automatic student recruitment machine for the institution as highly satisfied graduates or current students will most likely share the good news about the great learning experience. The graphical illustration below summarizes the various qualities that drive engagement [Figure 1].

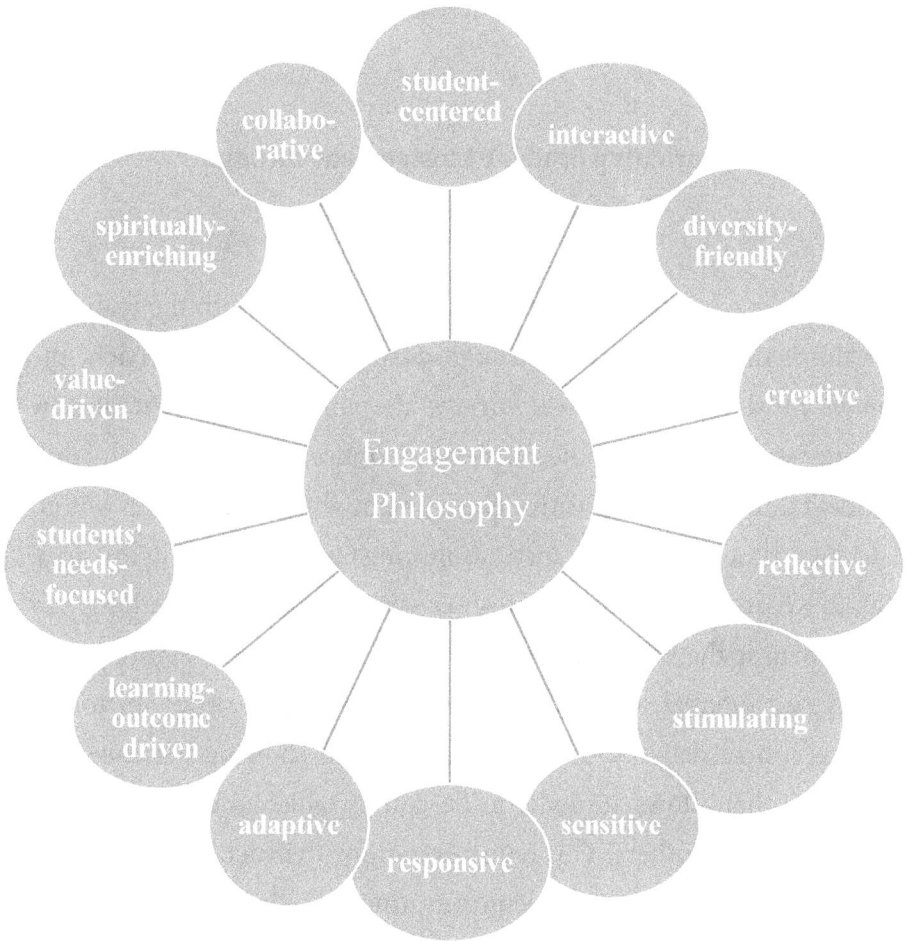

Figure 1. Qualities that Drive Engagement

The qualities in Figure 1 should be the bedrock of instructor-driven expectations. Every instructor should undergo a special training to imbibe the qualities that promote in and out of class engagement. If there is a strong positive correlation between engagement and performances in continuous learning activities (Rajabalee,

Santally, and Rennie, 2020), the focus should be on how to enrich engagement in order to ensure desirable performance and expected outcomes.

Enriching Student Engagement through
A Customer Service Approach

The sooner educational institutions come to terms with the reality of recruitment and retention through customer service approach, the better most institutions will survive the current onslaught of new online students. With the increasing options for potential adult students, the need for positive engagement with students will not go away anytime soon, hence, institutions must up their game in this area. Jakub Kliszczak's (2020) 15 customer service principles go a long way in deepening the level of engagement with students. See Figure 2.

A coordinated approach from the recruitment office up to the online course delivery should be uniform in showing patience and empathy that allows students to be comfortable enough to become vulnerable with others. This requires training instructors to treat each student as a customer while demonstrating the principles of customer service. The importance of instructor or facilitator's innovation and creativity is central in Sharoff's (2019) submission, especially one that grabs students' attention, captures their interest, gains their confidence, and drives their active involvement and participation in an atmosphere of freedom, tolerance, neutrality, and broad-mindedness. However, it should also be one of warmth, direct invitation to involve students in class activities, coupled with gentle prodding that shows the instructor's active presence and effectiveness.

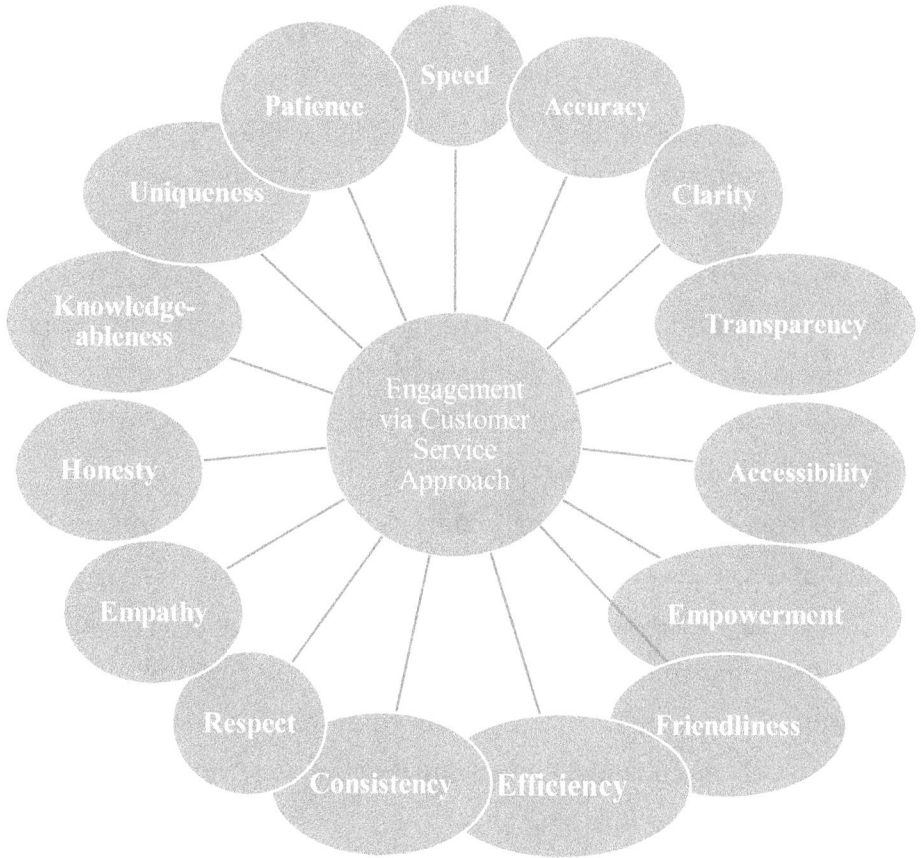

Figure 2. Kliszczak's (2020) 15 Customer Service Principles

From a hands-on experience, most students open up when an instructor writes them a personal email, shows empathy by giving student tips for success, accepts requests to go over the essay draft to see if the student is on the right path, and makes online classroom discussion forums less stressful by posing questions that are relevant to day-to-day life issues, as well as a few interesting questions with no right or wrong answers. Responses to students' inquiries should be within 24 hours while instructors simplify the course contents for easy comprehension, including the use of symbols, acronyms, and photos to simplify complex concepts and ideas. A friendly phone follow up or a faculty to student "friendly prompting" via a social media vehicle goes a long way, especially if it is to wish a student happy birthday, invite a student to check out a short video, or connect such students with few other students in a chat room about a current-life issue. Jamie Spencer (2019) submits that "people have always been looking for ways to connect and network with each other," and with the "age of digitization, people have found ways to be socially active on the internet, which is possible with the advent of the numerous social networking platforms and apps."

Through online learning, seminaries and university colleges can deploy social media platforms to implement Duncan and Duncan's (2019) "*10 golden rules of customer service*" in guiding and facilitating a deeper classroom engagement if the facilitator or the instructor adapts the customer service approach to sensitize, stimulate, and interact. Duncan and Duncan suggest the following will help in fostering a deeper engagement.

Golden Rule No 1: "If the customer comes first, there is a good chance the customer will come back" (Duncan and Duncan, 2019, xxiii) "Go beyond and beyond and beyond" (1). A zoom video call to inquire how a student is doing goes a long way in deepening engagement.

Golden Rule No 2: "The most effective and inexpensive advertising is a happy customer who tells the world about you, your product, and your company" (9). "Delight the customer every step of the way" (11). There should be a policy in place to resolve any student's concern within 24 hours, including setting up a hub where students and faculty can meet to engage on general issues. There should be another hub for one on one personal issues.

Golden Rule No. 3: "If you want business to get better for you, you have to get better at business" (19). "Make the milestones magical and memorable" (21). The use of social media to send birthday, anniversary, get-well soon, praying for you, you can do it encouragement notes, and other similar greetings connect students and instructor together in an enriching atmosphere.

Golden Rule No. 4: "If you want your customers for life, you need to talk to them during their lives" (31). "Serve" (33). A "help or needs" hub where students can freely share their academic struggles and challenges and subsequently get desired help within hours is one that will make the act of service contagious. This also encourages group work as well as student-to-student assistance.

Golden Rule No. 5: "Most people will use your service once. The key is to get them to use your service forever" (39). "Use over-the-top communication to WOW the customer" (41). Institutions can decide to break down a complex course idea into 20 words and intentionally share new ideas every week via few social media platforms that the student will likely see.

Golden Rule No. 6: "The law of the encore: The greater the performance, the louder the applause" (47). "Deliver the unexpected to create business karma" (49). An institution can generate weekly ideas that a student needs to integrate theory with practice and to share relevant ideas with two or three fellow students in supporting them in those areas of their lives.

Golden Rule No. 7: "Give your best to your best so you can get the rest of what they have to give you" (55). "Blow your customer away" (57). Faculty should never ambush students. Students should know expectations way ahead, and the pathway to satisfying those expectations should be visibly available for everyone to access. Faculty should think of doing something uncommon to show that the interests of students are paramount.

Golden Rule No. 8: "If you can't find the time to do it right, you will never find the time to do it over" (63). "Offer sizzling guarantees" (65). From the point of enrollment, the interests and best learning approaches of each student should guide the way everyone within the institution deal with each student. For instructors, assuring students of a successful completion based on the pathway on ground is key. Adapting the learning delivery option on the basis of each student's preference is also necessary to give students the guarantee of success. For example, a student who prefers to present an essay in a professionally recorded video instead of a long paper essay should have the option to do so.

Golden Rule No. 9: Get it right the first time, all the time, every time." (75). "Recover boldly" (77) – "a deep and sincere apology for the problem," "a quick commitment to a solution," "delivery of a solution that is more than expected," and "a follow-up to make sure everything is okay" (81). The guiding principle is to correct quickly any mistake, to the point that the students will personally express satisfaction before the case is finally put away.

Golden Rule No. 10: "When you have a service breakdown, the key is how fast and how well you recover the customer. Every second counts" (87). Make saying thank you a big-time event (89). The era of thinking that schools are doing students a favor is over. Institutions must thank students for selecting them rather than another one and for preferring them over others.

An institutional approach that puts customer service at the fore front prepares all institutional employees to treat every individual student in a way that promotes students' involvement and makes their classroom experience attractive, safe, conducive, inviting, and con-genial. From online forum discussions to online group chats, various online hubs—from writing skills to sharing personal and general concerns as well as spiritual experiences—schools should give high priority to sensitivity to students' needs and concerns while equally stimulating a creatively empowering in and out of class interaction. This is where instructors should wear their creative hearts. Asroff's (2020) study points out the importance of instructors training in the use of instructor-generated multimedia but giving such instructors the liberty to be creative throughout the semester in the use of the tools. Asroff emphasizes on the need to know and do what students find most engaging in order to guarantee "social presence, teaching presence, and cognitive presence" (5-A), and ultimately give students the best experience for success.

Pastoral Care Approach to Enriching Engagement

The five areas of pastoral care (The Scots College, 2017) can help enrich students' engagement.

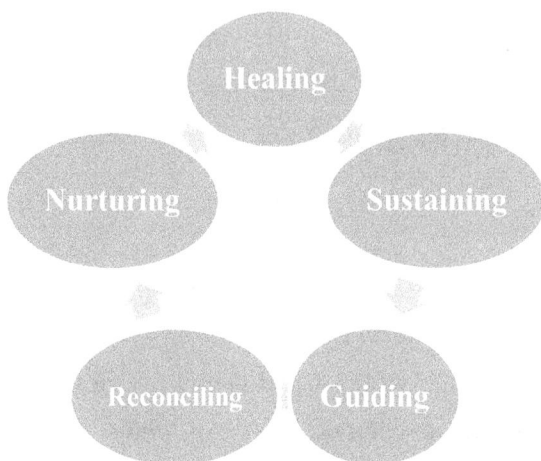

Figure 3. The five areas of pastoral care.

Empathy, active listening, acknowledgement of a real-life pain, enduring patience, and offering of prayers are some ways the healing and engaging function of online learning can take place. Many students come with personal baggage, and an institution's response can make or mar the learning experience of such students. Many students come into a program confused, and when institutions make extra effort to support and guide such students, the students can move from mere surviving to thriving. Sustaining such students can come in the form of helping them locate books and other materials they will need, showing them the skills of reading and writing an academic paper, and guiding them with approaches to discussion forum participation. Pastoral care mentality is never to assume that a student should know something. It helps to guide and guard students in such a way that they are able to know the various options available to them, including specific examples of expectations and connections with peers and tutors for maximum support.

The introduction of spiritual mentors based on students' preferences helps students grow spiritually, while promoting reconciliation and nourishment through the exercise of spiritual disciplines, practical service in the church, prayers, fasting, reading the word, practice of patience, and being hospitable. It also leads to an online group interaction of chapel experiences. Students can also share specific areas of service in order to bless others while lifting up the name of God. A special online hub can hold all of this with the specific goal of supporting the holistic growth and spiritual development of students.

An instructor with a pastoral care mentality comes to "class" unassuming with open-mindedness and with the expectation to hold the hand of the student in a cordial way that opens up the hearts of such students to learning, engaging, and thriving.

A Way to Philosophically Engender a Mentality Of Customer Service and Pastoral Care

A philosophy of distance/online education should drive the customer service and pastoral care mentality and chart the pathway in the delivery of a well-coordinated engagement playbook that leads to student satisfaction. Training and retraining should be continuous and ongoing.

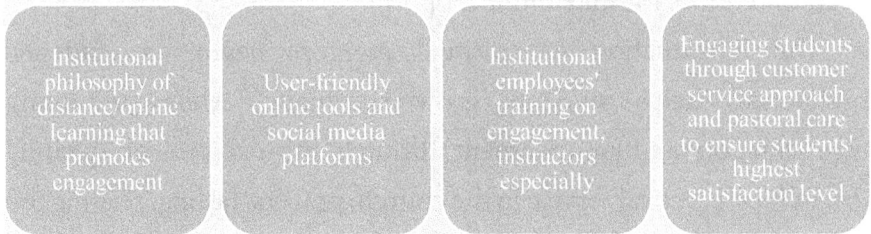

Figure 4. Institutional philosophy of a customer service approach

There should be an institutional synergy in the way the various aspects of the philosophy of distance/online education drive the kind of platforms the institution decides to use, the creativity the tools are put to, the way the institutions go about understanding each student (customer care in this case), and the pastoral care mentality the institution and their employees adopt to ensure a highly satisfying learning experience for every student. It is important for all institutional employees to realize that students' engagement starts from the day a prospect makes the phone call to inquire about enrollment to the day the student wears the graduation gown to cross the line during commencement. Hence, focus should be on achieving students' highest satisfaction level.

Some specific areas that an instructor may want to explore, though not exhaustive, is graphically illustrated in Figure 5.

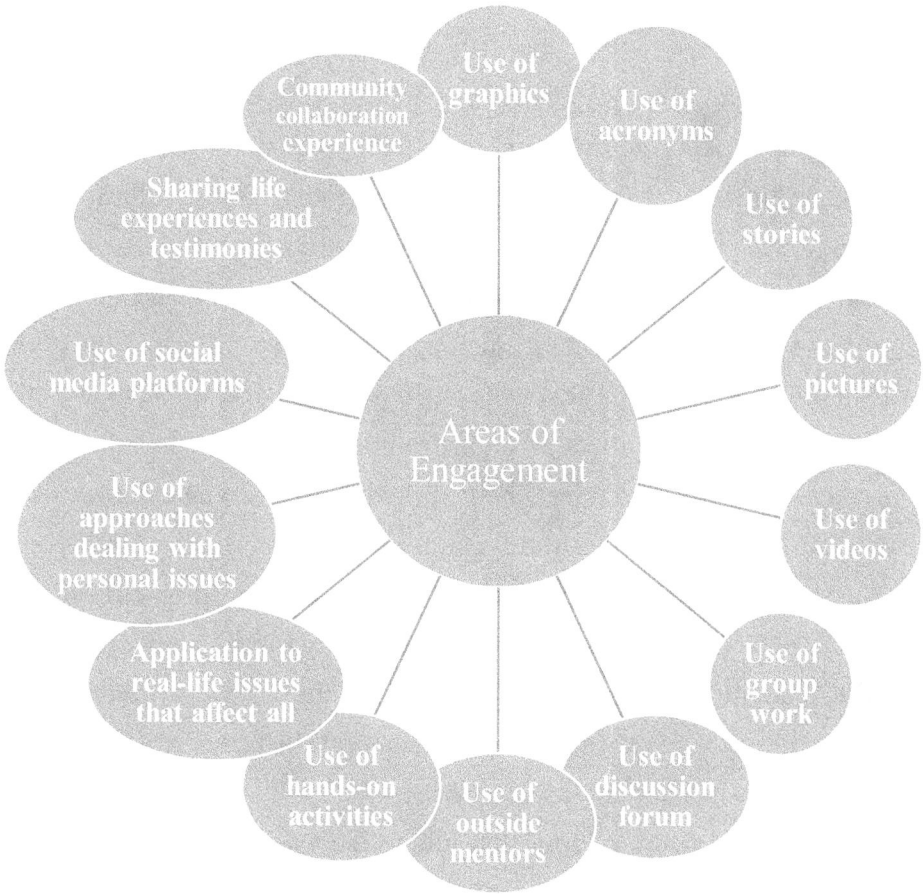

Figure 5. Areas of engagement.

The areas of engagement should form part of the focus of an instructor who wants to create an engaging classroom atmosphere where students can have a role to play without feeling any constraints.

Conclusion

It is essential to get instructors to buy into the ideals of class engagement. Also, getting to know students' learning preferences is another important thing we cannot ignore. Rios, Elliot and Mandernach (2018) call attention to the importance of the instructor's ability to know what and how students would like to learn online in order to guarantee student satisfaction. According to Rios et al. (2018), course design should be adaptable and easy to use, accessible, practical with easy and concise steps or instructions to follow. In addition, evaluations should that will help the student and engender closer rapport and communication, coupled with the opportunity for clarification of questions between the student and the instructor. Rios et al. (2018) conclude that students who interact more with contents, other students, and the instructor, as well as those fully involved with classroom activities are also more content, fulfilled, and satisfied with online courses. They are inspired to learn.

One should not assume that all students will find a particular approach to learning most appealing, no matter how well-intentioned the people that came up with the idea are. Swartzwelder, Murphy, and Murphy (2019) most likely expect to see more students in a nursing ethics course show preference for video-based discussion over the traditional text-based one, and when their research outcome did not go that way, they suggested that this could be due to familiarity with what the students are used to. It is necessary to state that the role of the instructor goes a long way in facilitating interaction. It includes knowing the best approach to get students' full attention, commitment, and productive involvement.

If it is by any stretch true that online learning does poorly in student-to-student collaboration and student-to-faculty exchanges opined by Paulsen and McCormick (2020), then one has to show keen interest in the way online learners can collaborate more and how instructors and learners can interact more, especially as online platforms have features to promote a higher level of student-to-student and students-to-instructor collaboration and interaction. The main issue comes back to the question: Do we have instructors that are well-trained to use the tools as well as have the necessary social skills backed by online philosophy of learning to make the tools most effective?

The importance of course content's relevance to reality is one major area online engagement must take into serious consideration. Among the many areas Martin and Bolliger's (2018) study identify, the relevance of course content to reality is non-negotiable; and this should go beyond the make-belief world of classroom work to "working on real-world projects" (205). Many students continue to find regular classrooms uninspiring as long as they have no relevance to their real world. Relevance to personal issues engenders engagement in this context.

Feeling connected to the instructor and the other students in and outside "the classroom," while actively playing an active part within the online learning experience, are two important areas this study identifies. Al-Dheleai and Tasir (2019), while investigating the perception of social presence on Web 2.0, affirm "that students engage in learning when they feel connected with others and when they play an active role in their learning process" (13). If this is so, facilitators and instructors have a huge role to play in ensuring the right connection and the right role to guarantee active involvement. Using graphics, acronyms, stories, pictures, videos, group work, discussion forum, outside mentors, hands-on activities, real-life issues that affect all, personal issues, testimonies, community collaboration experience, and social media platforms, while operating from a clearly understandable online education philosophy assist greatly in engendering a solid engagement in online learning.

References

Al-Dheleai, Y. M., and Tasir, Z. (2019). Web 2.0 for fostering students' social presence in online learning-based interaction. *Journal of Technology and Science Education, 9*(1), 13-19.

Asroff, C. L. (2020). The effect of instructor-generated multimedia on student engagement in online graduate. *Dissertation Abstracts International Section A: Humanities and Social Sciences, 81*(5-A).

DePietro, A. (2020). Here's a look at the impact of coronavirus (COVID-19) on colleges and universities in the U.S. Retrieved May 8, 2020 from https://www.forbes.com/sites/andrewdepietro/2020/04/30/impact-coronavirus-covid-19-colleges-universities/

Duncan, T., and Duncan, D. (2019). *The 10 golden rules of customer service.* Simple Truths.

Hutton, C., and Robson, J. (2019). Breaking barriers, building community: Improving student engagement with preparation for studying online multidisciplinary science by distance learning – A Case Study. *New Directions in the Teaching of Physical Sciences, 14*(1).

https://eric.ed.gov/contentdelivery/servlet/ERICServlet?accno=EJ 1231830

Kliszczak, J. (2020). 15 customer service principles you're not aware of. Channels. Retrieved May 10, 2020 from

https://www.channels.app/blog/customer-service-principles

Martin, F., and Bolliger, D. U. (2018). Engagement matters: Student perceptions on the importance of engagement strategies in the online learning environment. *Online Learning, 22*(1), 205-222.

Paulsen, J., and McCormick, A. C. (2020). Reassessing Disparities in Online Learner Student Engagement in Higher Education. *Educational Researcher, 49*(1).

Rajabalee, B. Y., Santally, M. I., and Rennie, F. (2020). A study of the relationship between students' engagement and their academic performances in an eLearning environment. *E-Learning and Digital Media, 17*(1).

Rios, T., Elliott, M., and Mandernach, B. J. (2018). Efficient instructional strategies for maximizing online student satisfaction. *Journal of Educators Online, 15*(3).

https://eric.ed.gov/contentdelivery/servlet/ERICServlet?accno=EJ 1199228

Sharoff, L. (2019). Creative and innovative online teaching strategies: Facilitation for active participation. *Journal of Educators Online, 16*(2). https://eric.ed.gov/contentdelivery/servlet/ERICServlet?accno=EJ 1223934

Spencer, J. (2019). 65+ social networking sites you need to know about. Retrieved May 3, 2020 from https://makeawebsitehub.com/social-media-sites/

Swartzwelder, K., Murphy, J., and Murphy, G. (2019). The impact of text-based and video discussions on student engagement and interactivity in an online course. *Journal of Educators Online, 16*(1). https://eric.ed.gov/contentdelivery/servlet/ERICServlet?accno=EJ 1204391

Tanner, T., and Smith Brown, E. (2015). Why 100 ATS member schools have grown. The Association of Theological Schools and The Commission on Accrediting. Retrieved May 9, 2020 from https://www.ats.edu/uploads/resources/publications-presentations/documents/why-100-schools-have-grown.pdf

The Scots College (2017). The five crucial functions of pastoral care. Retrieved February 8, 2020 from https://www.tsc.nsw.edu.au/tscnews/the-five-crucial-functions-of-pastoral-care

Toro-Troconis, M., Alexander, J., and Frutos-Perez, M. (2019). Assessing student engagement in online programmes: Using learning design and learning analytics. *International Journal of Higher Education, 8*(6), 171-183.

7

Steps toward Equitable Access for Faculty New to Online Learning

Lawrence Hopperton

There has been increasing attention to the issue of disability compliance in distributed learning over the past few years. While laws currently apply primarily to publicly funded institutions and have involved civil lawsuits, non-profits know that compliance is only a matter of time. Significant steps forward have been made in the last few years, particularly with courses that were designed and developed to be fully online. But many faculty, particularly those who teach in the classroom only, while familiar with the idea of accommodations for disabilities, are unaware of the process of compliance in online learning. This is because they believe that because they are classroom faculty, then all is well. And then the COVID-19 crisis hit. In the space of days, institutions went from wait and see to total shutdown and the transfer of all educational activity to internet applications.

In a current survey by Lederman (2020), 65% of faculty caught in the pandemic have no experience with online education. They make course adjustments on the fly. This is our only way to salvage the semester: shut down all on-ground classes and announce the transition to online; provide basic faculty training in online systems and methods; send in every technical help person to make it work. Online systems have been capable of scaling to support the surge rapid of users, but there are few roadmaps for inexperienced faculty who suddenly find themselves attempting to shoe-horn on-ground experience into an online environment that they know only at basic levels.

It has been an epic ride. In the new normal, everybody has had exposure to online education or at least computer supported learning. From spring, to summer, to fall, we have done our best in 2020. But as we battle onward, what are we leaving behind? Have the rights of our more challenged students been overlooked in the confusion of reactions? If fully robust, online courses have disability considerations built into their design and delivery, shouldn't these considerations not now be built into all courses that involve a distributed learning component? That is logical, and it is also the law.

Compliance in COVID-19

Compliance requirements under the American Disabilities Act (ADA) and the underlying Web Content Accessibility Guidelines (WCAG) specifications are very detailed and required progressively over three levels. Many of the requirements rely upon back-end systems or media production in order to produce alternative representations of content. As a faculty member who is new to all this, are there things that you can do to carry compliance forward, especially over the next few semesters, into the new normal. It would be unrealistic for an institution to require that all faculty meet compliance specifications in all courses within the short term. But there are simple steps that faculty can take while in the process of trying online learning that will establish a general level of consistency onto which institutions can build over time.

We are creatures of perception, and we tend to trust our own; however, for compliance, we need to think from the perspective of a person who needs accessibility considerations. That describes a huge population ranging from the physically to the cognitively challenged. And the ADA requires that we have accommodations in place before students register, rather than those put into place on a case-by-case basis. Much of this can be handled through system refinement such as adding criteria to student profiles that can adjust LMS settings (eg. File availability, adjusting time considerations on tests), but the core element is the content in the course. This needs to use some simple starting points in the creation of content elements in order to bring them to a basic level accessibility for assistive devices:

1. Text is king since it is a standard interface with assistive devices. The king of text is sans serif such as Helvetica or Colibri. Serif fonts have additional ornamentation at the ends of characters. These provide a level of distortion as they are received by assistive devices.

2. Provide multiple representations of content. A video or audio file is a content element. Captioning is an alternative representation. If an image or graphic presents content, a text description is an alternative.

Key areas for faculty to consider in building compliance into courses are audio/visual accessibility, document accessibility, and system accessibility.

Audio/Video Compliance

Audio/Visual accessibility refers to anything that requires hearing or eyesight. It refers to videos, slide images and pretty well everything that delivers content, and it requires that anything that is seen or heard is captioned, including audio that is part of a slide presentation. Text is king, remember, and a transcription is always the best alternative, but under the current laws, algorithmic captioning, even with misspellings and lack of punctuation, is considered to be sufficient for the next few years. Nevertheless, captions should still be inspected for accuracy since algorithmic misinterpretation can garble the meaning. Best practices would recommend either a manual process of caption correction or a commercial captioning service, both of which require sufficient lead time and budgets.

Slides

One of the most common visual inclusions is slides. These can contain other media elements, most commonly test, images, and often audio. In order to create accessible slides, there are some common sense styles that facilitate perception.

1. Use high contrast colours. Red on blue is difficult to see at the best of times due to low contrasts. Black on white provides the greatest contrast.

2. Limit the amount of text on each slide. If you supply a reference to a biblical text, you do not need to include the actual text. Headings are often sufficient.
3. Use clean backgrounds in order to avoid distractors and to steer perception to the content.
4. Use sans-serif fonts.

Images

Images, whether in slides or other documents, deserve special consideration. If an image is being used for decorative purposes rather than to convey content, you don't need to worry at all. But if an image does convey content, then it must be produced somewhat differently. This is consistent with the basic requirement for multiple represent-tations of content.

Content bearing images need texts that describes what the image is intended to convey. This text can either appear with the image or as a descriptive tag attached to the image. There will be more about tags later. Just remember that a content bearing image must have an alternative, text presentation.

Document Accessibility

Document accessibility can be a large topic but it begins with a few assumptions. In all likelihood, you are using standard document and office software. There are both default and user-selected settings within these programs that provide or change accessibility; for example, an institution can set a default font when computers are configured. Typically, this will be a sans-serif font that is consistent with ADA requirements. A user can change this, but it would not be advisable. Accessibility requirements specify that sans-serif fonts must be used. Serif fonts are more ornamental in their appearance, particularly at the ends of strokes, making the transmitted data more difficult for assistive devices to process and increasing chances to confound the message. This becomes an important point for other software defaults. Levels of headings is a perfect example.

Like many academics, when I write, I sit down and generate text. Then I revise and work to complete it. At the end, I worry about formatting. There are two choices. I can manually set my levels of headings, fonts, and colors. Alternatively, I can use the software defaults. The outcome may be visually identical, but only one can be interpreted by an assistive device. When we select a software default, that selection carries a hidden tag that communicates to assistive devices and provides interpretive details for what is coming next. These tags are not included when you self-set your headings.

Taking this the logical step further, when you bring tables, images, or other inclusions into your document, ensure that your final formatting of the piece follows system defaults since these embed the tags for assistive devices. These are the same tags mentioned regarding slides. Tags are embedded code that provides information that can be interpreted by an assistive device.

Finally, we should address PDF documents. We assume that what we have produced is identical to what our students have received. Remember tags? If you save a document as PDF, it will not carry compliance tags. But if you export it as a PDF, you will have a choice of using a compliance checkbox.

There are two reminders:

1. Hyperlinks: If you are going to embed a hyperlink in a document, provide the link with a descriptive label, rather than "click here."
2. Color. These are not always visible. If possible, do not use color to communicate content, and if you do, tag it with a text explanation. Similarly, when using system defaults in your learning management system, communication tags for assistive devices are added automatically. Your LMS administrator should be able to adjust system defaults in order to enhance contrast, but this does not negate the warning about color usage. Red is red if you can see it. Black on white is always the best.

There is a checklist for this next step towards accessibility in education and for the stage we are at right now, it is fairly obvious:

1. Text is king.
2. Provide multiple representations of content.
3. Use software defaults and sans-serif fonts.
4. Use LMS system defaults.
5. Caption all recorded audio/video files.

It is April, 2020, while I write this. All classes for the summer are online. We don't yet know about September 2020. We are waiting and planning. Computers are campuses, conference rooms, office hours, and coffee meetings, at least for now. We are a constituency that can carry education forward, embracing accessibility into common design and development. Progress will be incremental, and the suggestions here are intended to bring us to a common standard for building accessible education. It is a matter of time before all institutions will be required to be complaint. As we face the required shift to online learning and the associated creation of curriculum, this is the time for a mindset of compliance, rather than just a checklist, to become part of our ordinary activities.

Reference

Lederman, D. (2020) How teaching changed in the (forced) shift to remote learning. *Inside Higher Education*, April 22.

8

Actively Engaging the Remote-Learner

Matthew Boutilier

Introduction

Picture yourself in front of your computer screen. You sit back in your leather, overstuffed office chair, lean your head back and take a sip of your coffee. You login to your remote class and visit a few discussion forum posts or check out a few assignments. Yet, your "classroom" is eerily silent. No one raises a hand. No small talk or any other type of conversation. No dialogue with any of the students. No questions to ask them to get them to engage in the readings you've assigned. The one deafening sound you hear is *silence*. Yet, that silence communicates a lot of information to you. But you are not sure whether or not it is telling you the truth or something entirely different. It tells you that your students are not interested in the video you just shared with them. Or, that they are not reading the feedback you spent so much time sharing with them on the project they just submitted last week. Or, that you just aren't cut out for remote teaching at all...

Is that how you feel? Are all of these voices speaking in your head and you really aren't sure what to believe? Can you really do this? How do you really know whether or not you are doing a good job? If you have never taught a remote course before, many of these questions could be plaguing your mind. It can be very unsettling not to know how you stand in your class. But, don't feel as though you have no way of knowing. Or, that you have little or no control over being successful in teaching your remote class. Taking classes from a distance has come a long way from being glorified correspondence courses to effective ways for students to learn and grow and be engaged with the content, with their classmates, and even their instructors.

One of the first things anyone encounters when attempting to teach in a remote environment is the lack of physical presence. Before entering this new educational space, this obvious difference does not appear to be all that significant. Yet, when you first enter that space that fact becomes deafening. The social interactivity of the physical classroom, the natural give-and-take of a lively discussion around some fascinating topic, or the nonverbal feedback you receive from students during a lecture are no longer givens in a remote context.

You may have asked yourself how can a remote classroom be interactive? How can I as the professor engage my students? How can students actually learn in a remote environment? Well, there is hope not only in the fact that others have successfully done it, but that you can do it, too. One of the things that makes something unfamiliar seem impossible is its *unfamiliarity.* If you can remember back to before you were able to drive a car, you probably had some ideas visualized in your head as to how driving would feel. You may have overthought several of the things you would need to do and be aware of in order to drive a car safely. Now that you are a veteran driver, you probably do not consciously think about many of those things anymore because driving has almost become second nature to you. You hop in the driver's seat, turn the key, put the vehicle in drive, and away you go without too much thought.

Now, think about yourself teaching a remote class for the first time. There are many unknowns. Perhaps you have a lot of presuppositions about what you anticipate the experience will be like. You may have heard some horror stories from others about what it was like for them. Or, perhaps you may have some bad experiences yourself. But, just like many other things in life, the more you know about something and the better you can prepare ahead for it, the better that experience can be. And, who knows? You may even enjoy it. Perhaps, you may even look forward to it.

The Differences between
Traditional, Remote, and Remote Learning

Lack of Physical Presence

Let us begin with the elephant in the room. One of the more obvious things you notice that is missing in a remote class is the lack of physical presence. Your students are not sitting in front of you in the class. This creates a very different dynamic than if you had them in the same physical location. You no longer have the keen ability to "read the room." As you are talking or asking questions, you cannot sense from the looks of your students' faces whether or not they are tracking with you or not. Therefore, it is imperative for remote instructors to create community with their students intentionally.

Community does not just happen. Conditions must be met in order to initiate, establish, and maintain a robust virtual community.[1] It is critical that the instructor be proactive in establishing a virtual learning community at the beginning of the course (Slagter van Tryon and Bishop, 2009, 304). Acknowledging that remote learning may be intimidating to many, when one takes the initiative to provide some ways to ease that anxiety, it will go a long way to reduce stress for the student (Lehman and Conceição, 2010, 40). Developing an authentic community in a remote learning environment is a collaborative effort (Lehman and Conceição, 2010, 27–28; Anderson et al. 2001, 4). It is not the sole responsibility of the course instructor to develop and maintain this sense of community in a remote classroom. The instructor should solicit the assistance of an instructional designer or others who are tasked with best practices in integrating technology with pedagogical best practices within virtual environments. It is important to create ways to achieve a sense of *community*. Students may experience feelings of isolation and a lack of connection to their fellow students or their instructor in a remote learning environment. Therefore, efforts should be made to create an authentic sense of community where students feel they are connected with one another.

---

[1]Conditions that can provide an enhanced remote social community would include: **Social cues** describe a learner's perception of the personal emotions in remote classrooms (Chen and Chiu, 2008, 682). **Co-presence** describes how a remote learner feels a sense of "togetherness" with their fellow students and virtual community and feels as though they have the ability to engage in immediate communication (Zhao, 2003, 446). **Learning interactions** are those general social learning activities that enhance higher-level learning within a remote course (Offir and Lev, 2000, 1176).

Students who are a part of a learning community feel a sense of connection with their classmates and instructor. A shared sense of community creates mutual trust. Trust is beneficial in this environment as it helps students feel comfortable sharing with one another. When they share, there is a greater likelihood of learning. Students feel the freedom to explore together, to reflect together, and to share their findings, ask questions, etc. And, don't forget the informal social opportunities for learning. Learning occurs outside of the virtual classroom as well. Encourage your students to meet offline. Provide them with opportunities to develop relationships while at a distance. This can easily be accomplished by creating discussion forums, encouraging your students to meet via Zoom, Google Hangouts Meet, FaceTime, etc.

The instructor needs to think proactively through how to establish this community and maintain it, so their students experience authentic learning. Learning does not just happen in the classroom, physical or virtual. Authentic learning occurs as students have opportunities to ingest material, process it, reflect upon it, and discuss it within a community setting where they feel they can trust the others. What we want to do in our remote learning environments is to design these spaces to encourage such conversations to take place. Getting students to engage in a remote learning environment is crucial to the establishment and maintenance of an effective community network.

Research conducted by Kuh, Laird, and Umbach (2004, 26) highlighted some areas in which instructors facilitated student engagement. These included a higher level of interaction with students, facilitating more collaborative means for students to engage together with the content, as well as providing students with feedback that would benefit them moving forward. Achieving a level of interactivity within a remote course significantly correlates with increased learning outcome achievement among learners (Bernard et al., 2004, 411–412). This is dependent upon the ability of the students to be able to represent themselves as real people, which in turn requires students to participate in discussions and be "heard" by their classmates (Arbaugh, 2005, 139). Creating collaborative projects where students work interdependently with one another enables these sorts of meaningful interactions to occur (Lightner, Bober, and Willi, 2007, 8). When an effectively designed collaborative project is designed where students are allowed to construct something with their peers and are given the opportunity to evaluate and review one another's work, an authentic community can be achieved where students become highly engaged in their work (Miers et al., 2007, 538).

For participants in a virtual environment to feel comfortable interacting with one another, they need to feel that the environment was not contrived, where they felt their distance was no longer a factor and they actually "felt" they were physically present (Biocca, Harms, and Burgoon, 2003, 459). One way this can be accomplished is by developing effective ice-breaker activities at the beginning of a remote course as an informal pathway to become comfortable with the remote learning experience and begin the initial community development process (Herrington, Reeves, and Oliver, 2009, 135). It is also important during the beginning of the course for instructors to be sensitive and proactive when they notice students declining in activity. This silence can signify a sense of despair and a lack of efficacy in their ability to be successful in the remote environment. Since lack of visibility was an authentic concern in a remote context, providing formative ways to assess challenge areas for students in order to respond effectively so students can quickly get back on track is important (Vonderwell and Boboc, 2013). When learners experience community within their class, authentic learning takes place (Rovai, 2002, 328).

The type of social connection being sought to create community is one where instructors and students connect interdependently with one another and with the content at a deeper level. Instructors and instructional designers must look for ways to make the course content meaningful to students and provide ways to get the students engaged in the content so they are excited about it, intrinsically motivated to interact with it, and want to discuss it further (Schunk, Pintrich, and Meece, 2014, 238).

Creating a rich learning community in a remote learning context involves establishing three types of presence[2]: *social presence, cognitive presence, and teaching presence. Social presence* describes the interconnectivity of the group (Akyol and Garrison, 2008, 4). It is how a class gels and formulates. The group experiences the confidence to communicate openly and freely with one another. Relationships are developed. Authentic social presence possesses the ability to establish and maintain genuine, uninhibited interactions with one's virtual peers (Kehrwald, 2008, 94). Social presence brings a bond to the grouThere is an "intimate" sense of identification which garners certain aspects of influence between members (Rogers and Lea 2005, 151–152). Particularly significant for a remote context is the fact that members do not need to be in physical proximity to experience a

---

[2] "Presence is defined as a dynamic interplay between thought, emotion, and behavior" (Lehman and Conceição, 2010, 4).

heightened level of social presence. Rather, all that is necessary for the group members is to identify themselves authentically with the group (Rogers and Lea, 2005, 153). As social presence develops, students begin to achieve higher levels of meaningful interactions with one another (Garrison and Arbaugh, 2007). Social presence is progressive in the sense that the members develop a sense of sharing a common academic goal. This goal further solidifies the bond the members have with one another (Garrison and Arbaugh, 2007; Dixson, Kuhlhorst, and Reiff, 2006).

Social presence must move beyond just the establishment of interpersonal relationships if it is going to impact learning. These connections must involve group cohesion which requires intellectual focus and respect (Garrison and Arbaugh, 2007, 160). Other learners are essential to a robust social learning community in that they bring to the table diverse experiences and backgrounds (Beaudoin, 2002, 152–153). Therefore, it is essential to find creative ways to get learners engaged so they feel comfortable and confident to share these experiences within the virtual community. Support provided by the instructor is critical in alleviating fear and anxiety for remote students and is key in establishing a sense of presence (Lehman and Conceição, 2010, 26). Collaborative interaction with others in a learning environment allows learners to develop, wrestle with, and expand upon their limited knowledge and understanding of the material (Lehman and Conceição, 2010, 6–7). The give-and-take of ongoing discussion and debate of topics motivates learners to challenge their ideas and reframe or even reject their original conclusions. As a group begins to gel, students experience heightened engagement, which describes learners who are deeply involved in the learning environment together as they feel a real sense of belonging in their interactions with one another in their learning environment ((Lehman and Conceição, 2010, 4). Students develop a sense of satisfaction in their remote courses when they feel that social presence has been established, which leads to greater achievement of learning outcomes (Williams, Duray, and Reddy, 2006, 610; Arbaugh and Benbunan-Finch, 2006, 444).

Cognitive presence describes the ability for a learner to develop meaning through a personal iterative process and social interaction (Akyol and Garrison 2008, 4; Anderson et al. 2001, 10–11). When higher levels of social presence are experienced, higher levels of cognitive presence are also reported. As learners feel more comfortable in their learning environment where their instructor is modeling the way by making the interactive portions of the remote learning experience authentic and meaningful, learners report enhanced cognitive presence (Shea and Bidjerano, 2009, 551). In order for this to occur, the instructor must be intentional to ensure the learners feel a sense of comfort in their remote surroundings. Remote learners report that when efforts are made for them to get to know their peers and feel comfortable with them in their virtual learning environment, significant progress is reported as it pertains to cognitive presence (Shea and Bidjerano, 2009, 552). Cognitive presence is often closely associated with higher-order critical thought and student achievement (Garrison, Anderson, and Archer 1999, 89; Shea and Bidjerano 2009, 545). Instructors are significant facilitators of discussion if cognitive presence is to be attained (Meyer 2003, 57). Therefore, they must be intentional in how they design their assignments so as to create this type of learning environment (Meyer

2003, 63–64). The progression of developing cognitive presence involves the following stages (Anderson et al., 2001, 10–11):

1. The *triggering event* describes the identification of a problem that has been brought to the surface where the individual decides to initiate further investigation. To assist the learner in this initial stage, it is important for the proactive instructor to be attentive to guide, but not too closely and to steer the learner away from any potential distractions.

2. The *exploration stage* describes the stage where the learner begins to bring to the table past experiences to reflect upon as well as beginning to develop further inquiry about the situation at hand within the social learning context.

3. The *integration stage* describes the place where the learner has begun to develop some meaning from the exploratory process. As the pieces are being brought together, they begin to take shape and begin to make sense to the learner as they begin to reflect the initial problem posed earlier. As an iterative process, the learner may not only have questions resolved but also may have earlier understandings negated.

4. The *resolution stage* identifies the state where the learner has the opportunity to apply and successfully test their hypotheses that have developed as they have researched their identified problem.

Third, *teaching presence* is the structured design of "cognitive and social processes" for students to achieve success in their remote course

(Garrison, 2011; Akyol and Garrison, 2008, 4). Teaching presence describes the instructor's ability to achieve learning outcomes by designing constructive learning activities that utilize socially collaborative and critical thought (Garrison and Arbaugh, 2007). This draws on the significance of developing an effective social presence. The instructor plays a primary role in how their learners perceive their remote course. This is true not only because of its inherent value but because in order to develop effective cognitive and teaching presence, one needs a firm foundation of social presence, to begin with (Garrison and Arbaugh, 2007). Intentional and consistent faculty presence creates a bonding community in traditional and remote learning environments (Boettcher and Conrad, 2010, 38). Well-designed and effective remote courses facilitate consistent interaction between student, teacher, and content (Coffin Murray et al., 2012, 137). Research supports that the facilitator of a remote course has a tremendous influence on how their students perceive (either positively or negatively) their virtual learning environment (Oncu and Cakir, 2011, 1100).

One of the most powerful tools remote instructors have at their disposal to maintain a sense of teaching presence is providing *evaluative feedback* (Coffin Murray et al., 2012, 137). Evaluative feedback is an effective social process that helps students improve their work. Research conducted by Kuh, Laird, and Umbach (2004, 28) indicates that instructors have influence on how their students perform. For example, if the instructor deems an activity important and provides feedback to assist in their success, students equate it as an integral part of the overall learning process with a higher level of engagement. When instructors design a variety of learning activities for students, this proves to be a contributing factor in learning outcome achievement as learners are more engaged in such activities (Kuh, Laird, and Umbach, 2004, 29). The impact of teaching presence is critical to the degree that it is related to "student satisfaction, perceived learning, and a sense of community" (Garrison and Arbaugh, 2007).

Teaching presence is essential to balance cognitive and social issues consistent with the intended educational outcomes (Garrison, Anderson, and Archer, 1999). While these outcomes may result from the active leadership of a formally designated teacher, teaching presence goes beyond this individual and may be provided by any of the participants in the learning environment as all take on the role of the teacher (Garrison and Akyol, 2013, 85).

Effective Virtual Communication

Another critical component which actively engages remote learners is effective communication. Stimulating communication which involves learners who understand the direction of the virtual conversation and are active in its contribution rather than being passive receivers demonstrate higher learning outcome achievement as well as increased levels of student satisfaction (Lehman and Conceição, 2010, 5–6; Kang and Im, 2013, 299). As we have discussed, the lack of physical presence in a remote environment creates unique obstacles. One of those obstacles involves how we communicate with our students. Much of our communication in the physical classroom is taken for granted. This creates an eerie silence in our remote classroom. Communication occurs differently, but just because we are not located in the same physical place does not mean that communication does not take place. It is just different. There are several things to consider for an effective conversation, discussion, or debate with someone within a remote environment.

When we transition into a remote learning environment, we have to compensate for the lack of non-verbal ways of communicating. Whether we realize it or not, we communicate a lot without words (Adler and Rodman, 2006, 155). The facial expressions we use, the hand gestures used to make a point, and even the tone used while speaking all add depth to what we are saying (Adler and Rodman, 2006, 168–179). So, in a virtual environment, we need to take extra steps to make sure we recognize how our non-verbal communication that may be silenced by the lack of physical presence. We replace non-verbal by being in constant contact with our students. We need to be sure to follow-up with our students to make sure the message they received was the one we intended to send. We need to ask them to demonstrate they understand our meaning.

Another crucial piece we need to remember as it pertains to our communication within the remote learning environment is that we need to "over communicate." Be redundant! The students who are enrolled in remote classes are not *willing* virtual students who already know what to expect and have signed up for an online class. Students in a remote context may be newcomers to a virtual context. As faculty, we need to take the initiative not only to communicate clearly our expectations but also to repeat those expectations numerous times and in numerous places to make sure our students have access to the information they need.

Healthy environments characterized by rich conversations do not just happen. It is important that we create a space where students feel comfortable interacting with one another. If they feel comfortable, they are much more likely to share things of value and significance when in robust conversations. The best conversations in a face-to-face classroom are where there is ongoing dialogue among students who give-and-take in the exchange. In a typical face-to-face learning environment, there are few things more special than participating in a meaningful exchange about ideas and concepts that hold interest. The give-and-take in such a dialogue make our hearts pump a little faster and puts us at the edge of our seats. But what happens when the students and the professor are miles apart typing on a keyboard in response to what someone else has posted on a discussion forum thread hours ago? The excitement and enthusiasm shared by someone has long faded. The motivation initiated by the student has long been forgotten. The time distance is a real enemy of remote learning. As the instructor, we need to be present even when we are not "present." What I mean by that is that we need to be intentional about the way in which we interact in those synchronous forums. We need to think creatively and be sure to express passionate enthusiasm so that even if the post or video is read or viewed at a later time the passion and enthusiasm fades little.

Furthermore, students need to feel safe to talk, discuss, share, offer opinions, and freely give and receive constructive feedback (Edmondson, 2012, 118). This needs to happen without fear of harsh criticism or retribution for what they share openly and publicly. Although such environments cannot be forcefully constructed, leaders can take initiative to create the parameters necessary to encourage this healthy environment (Edmondson, 2012, 124).

Types of Student Engagement

All remote courses need to be designed and taught in a way to increase student engagement. We want to understand how we can connect with our students so they can connect deeply with the subject matter to learn. We not only want them to learn the course materials so they perform well on exams during the course, we also want them to take what they learn and be able to apply that deep knowledge into their future courses and more importantly, to various contexts long after they leave our course. We want to guide them to connect the logical dots from the content to life beyond our virtual classroom. In order to do so, we need to be intentional about creatively constructing opportunities for students to engage with one another, with the content, and with the instructor. Authentic learning comprises all three types of student engagement, and we cannot settle with only one or two.

Student-Content Engagement

The window to learning is the student's exposure to the *content*. Initially, we want to be sure that we create an effective environment for our students to engage actively in the course materials. We need to do more than require our students to read the text and answer some questions to verify their comprehension of the reading. We need to make it relevant to them. We must go the extra mile or two to connect what they already know with where we want them to be. This involves providing solid content students can understand, reflect on, and connect with. Are there things in the current media today that can easily connect with the content to demonstrate to students how a better understanding of the content can help them process those things better and perhaps help to change it for the better? Are there multiple media through which to share the content of the materials? What digital tools could help students reflect and sharpen their critical thinking skills? How can we help our students not focus on the "right" answers but take steps to process and arrive at conclusions? Getting from point A to point B is rarely a straight line.

Student-Instructor Engagement

To enhance authentic learning in a remote environment, the instructor needs to be sure to provide opportunities to support the student in their learning. As instructors, we need to be sure to exercise skill in connecting with our students to know when they need support and the best way to deliver that support. Support should come in the way of identifying where the student is and helping them to get to the next point on the journey. It does not mean we carry them on our shoulders. What it does mean is that we invest in them by providing them critical feedback. Authentic and honest feedback is a necessary element in our student's learning. Feedback demonstrates to our students that we care and that we will encourage them to have internal motivation necessary for them to succeed, not only in our class, but in other classes and in their vocational endeavors once they graduate. This feedback does not just merely comment on what the student has done wrong. Rather, and more importantly, it provides helpful insights as to why students get things wrong and how they can go about correcting the errors. The purpose is not just to provide a correct answer, but also to assess the rationale and the root cause of the error in order to correct the thought processes that led to it. Then, students can address those errors to understand how they should perform better the next time (Garrison, 2011; Akyol and Garrison, 2008, 4). We can also support students by embedding formative assessment measures to make sure they are on the right track and they are keeping up with the material. The assessments do not need to be complex. They can ask the students just a few questions to gauge quickly their comprehension of the necessary elements of the material for the week, so they are more likely to be successful as the course continues.

Engaging your students in this way also includes initiating conversations with them. We show we care by asking how they are doing, praying for them, and by being there for them. Virtual education is challenging in the sense that we are not physically present with your students. Therefore, we are less likely to know what is going on in their lives. We can change that. We can be sure that we make ourselves available by hosting virtual office hours, hosting live discussions using a video conferencing application (Zoom Meetings, Google Hangouts Meet), or by sending them a message to check in on them.

Another means of showing we care is to host a "meet and greet" session at the very beginning of your class. This demonstrates care and concern for our students at the beginning of the semester. During the meet and greet, we invite our students to a live video conference meeting. The agenda is pretty straight forward. We begin the time by just a round of introductions. Then, we provide a brief overview of the syllabus and the course in general with our expectations and how we plan to grade their work. The underlying purpose behind this is to get to know our students and for our students to get to know us as well as the other students. Then, it is important for us to maintain a consistent level of communication with our students so the students feel cared for and supported (Moore, 1989, 2).

Student-Student Engagement

Finally, in order to maintain an authentic remote learning environment, one must design the virtual learning environment so that there are genuine opportunities for students to engage with one another. Just as the prior types of engagement were designed to facilitate robust learning, so the design of student-student engagement needs to facilitate opportunities for students to learn from one another as they interact (Moore, 1989, 2). It is important for the instructor to create assessments where students collaborate together and nudge them to interact with, engage with, and rely upon one another in a team environment. This represents an authentic environment in which they will find themselves once they graduate and work in their vocation. As educators, we need to support students in a safe environment to enable them to learn from their mistakes and learn how to function in social environments, and to understand how to ask questions, how to give and receive feedback, how to disagree graciously, and how to execute plans.

Conclusion

Actively engaging remote learners comes down to seeking out ways to connect with them at a high level. Building an engaging, thriving learning environment where students benefit from a social learning community is the key to a successful remote learning environment. Authentic learning does not exist in a vacuum. We all learn through processing and reflecting on content by ourselves as well as interacting with others as we ask questions, debate perspectives, and sharpen ideas based on incorporating pieces of knowledge we picked up during those reflections and interactions. These moments of reflection and interaction with subject matter and other classmates compose the hallmark of learning. Much of this process is taken for granted in the traditional, face-to-face environments. Without the obvious physical presence, we may conclude that it is impossible to recreate the same type of learning atmosphere in our remote classes. Even though there are many differences, we can adapt the way we teach and engineer our methodology so that our students can still benefit from a highly engaging course even though they may be miles apart from one another and their instructor.

By being intentional about recognizing and establishing community in the remote classroom, we as instructors can successfully engage our students. Being sensitive to the fact that students learn in a social community speaks volumes as to how we need to design safe, effective, learning environments for our students. These decisions will drive our decisions about how content delivery, learning activities, assessment strategies, how assignments are evaluated, and how well we communicate expectations to our students. These elements are critical in traditional classrooms but become more evident in a remote environment. We should make every effort to engage our students, even though they may be miles apart.

References

Adler, R. B., and Rodman, G. R. (2006). *Understanding human communication.* 9th ed. New York: Oxford University Press.

Akyol, Z., and Garrison, D. R. (2008). The Development of a community of inquiry over time in an online course: Understanding the progression and integration of social, cognitive and teaching presence. *Journal of Asynchronous Learning Networks 12*(December), 3–22.

Anderson, T., Liam, R., Garrison, D. R., and Archer, W. (2001). Assessing teaching presence in a computer conferencing context. *5*(2), 1–17.

Arbaugh, J. B. (2005). Is there an optimal design for on-line MBA courses?" *Academy of Management Learning and Education 4*(2), 135–49.

Arbaugh, J. B., and Benbunan-Finch, R. (2006). An investigation of epistemological and social dimensions of teaching in online learning environments. *Academy of Management Learning and Education 5*(4), 435–47.

Beaudoin, M. F. 2002. "Learning or Lurking?" *The Internet and Higher Education 5*(2), 147–55.

Bernard, R. M., Abrami, P. C., Lou, Y., Borokhovski, E., Wade, A., Wozney, L., Wallet, P. A., Fiset, M., and Huang, B. (2004). How does distance education compare with classroom instruction? A meta-analysis of the empirical literature. *Review of Educational Research 74*(3), 379–439.

Biocca, F., Harms, C. and Burgoon, J. K. (2003). Toward a more robust theory and measure of social presence: Review and suggested criteria. *Presence: Teleoperators and Virtual Environments 12*(5), 456–80.

Boettcher, J. V., and Conrad, R.M. (2010). *The online teaching survival guide: Simple and practical pedagogical tips.* First. San Francisco: John Wiley and Sons.

Chen, G., and Chiu, M.M. (2008). Online discussion processes: Effects of earlier messages' evaluations, knowledge content, social cues and personal information on later messages. *Computers and Education 50*(3), 678–92.

Dixson, M., Kuhlhorst, M., and Reiff, A. (2006). Creating effective online discussions: Optimal instructor and student roles. *Journal of Asynchronous Learning Networks 10*(4), 15–28.

Edmondson, A. (2012). *Teaming: How organizations learn, innovate, and compete in the knowledge economy.* San Francisco, CA: John Wiley and Sons.

Garrison, D. R., and Akyol, Z. (2013). Toward the development of a metacognition construct for communities of inquiry. *The Internet and Higher Education 17*(April), 84–89.

Garrison, D. R. (2011). *E-learning in the 21st century: A framework for research and practice.* 2nd ed. New York: Taylor and Francis.

Garrison, D. R., and Arbaugh, J. B. (2007). Researching the community of inquiry framework: Review, issues, and future directions. *The Internet and Higher Education 10*(3), 157–72.

Garrison, D. R., Anderson, T., and Archer, W. (1999). Critical inquiry in a text-based environment: Computer conferencing in higher education. *The Internet and Higher Education 2*(2–3), 87–105.

Herrington, J., Reeves, T. C., and Oliver, R. (2009). *A practical guide to authentic e-learning.* Routledge.

Kang, M., and Im, T. (2013). Factors of learner-instructor interaction which predict perceived learning outcomes in online learning environment: Factors of learner-instructor interaction. *Journal of Computer Assisted Learning 29*(3), 292–301.

Kehrwald, B. (2008). Understanding social presence in text-based online learning environments. *Distance Education 29*(1), 89–106.

Kuh, G. D., Laird, T. F. N., and Umbach, P. D. (2004). Aligning faculty activities and student behavior. *Liberal Education 90*(4), 24–31.

Lehman, R. M., and Conceição, S. C. O. (2010). *Creating a sense of presence in online teaching: How to "be there" for distance learners.* San Francisco: John Wiley and Sons.

Lightner, S., Bober, M. J., and Willi, C. (2007). Team-based activities to promote engaged learning. *College Teaching 55*(1), 5–18.

Meyer, K. A. (2003). Face-to-face versus threaded discussions: The role of time and higher-order thinking. *Journal of Asynchronous Learning Networks 7*(3).

Miers, M. E., Clarke, B. A., Pollard, K. C., Rickaby, C. E., Thomas, J., and Turtle, A. (2007). Online interprofessional learning: The student experience. *Journal of Interprofessional Care 21*(5), 529–42.

Moore, M. G. (1989). Editorial: Three types of interaction. *American Journal of Distance Education 3*(2), 1–7.

Murray, M., Pérez, J., Geist, D., and Hedrick, A. (2012). Student interaction with online course content: Build it and they might come. *Journal of Information Technology Education 11*, 125–140.

Offir, B., and Lev, J. (2000). Constructing an aid for evaluating teacher-learner interaction in distance learning. *Educational Media International 37*(2), 91–97.

Oncu, S., and Cakir, H. (2011). Research in online learning environments: Priorities and methodologies. *Computers and Education 57*(1), 1098–1108.

Rogers, P, and Lea, M. (2005). Social presence in distributed group environments: The role of social identity. *Behaviour and Information Technology 24*(2), 151–58.

Rovai, A. (2002). Sense of community, perceived cognitive learning, and persistence in asynchronous learning networks." *The Internet and Higher Education 5*(4), 319–32.

Schunk, D. H., Pintrich, P. R., and Meece, J. (2014). Intrinsic motivation. In *Motivation in Education: Theory, Research, and Applications*, 4th ed. Boston: Pearson.

Shea, P., and Bidjerano, T. (2009). Community of inquiry as a theoretical framework to foster 'epistemic engagement' and 'cognitive presence' in online education. *Computers and Education 52*(3), 543–53.

Slagter van Tryon, P. J., and Bisho, M.J. (2009). Theoretical foundations for enhancing social connectedness in online learning environments. *Distance Education 30*(3), 291–315.

Vonderwell, S. K., and Boboc, M. (2013). Promoting formative assessment in online teaching and learning. *TechTrends 57*(4): 22–27.

Williams, E. A., Duray, R., and Reddy, V. (2006). Teamwork orientation, group cohesiveness, and student learning: A study of the use of teams in online distance education. *Journal of Management Education 30*(4), 592–616.

Zhao, S. (2003). Toward a taxonomy of copresence. *Presence: Teleoperators and Virtual Environments 12*(5), 445–55.

9

Facilitating Learner-Centered Online Education

Lawrence Hopperton

Introduction

Lev Vygotsky argued that learning is embedded in a social process of knowledge construction, rather than being an individual activity (Vygotsky, 1978). The processes and the outcomes in collaborative learning are strongly shaped by joint activity and interaction by the participants—including the course facilitator. Learning is not just an individual issue; rather, it is a matter of participating in the community of learners by helping to create new knowledge and to offer new ideas for scrutiny to their learning peers (Scaramalia and Bereiter, 2003). In other words, the process of developing individual capacity is based upon active, and interactive engagement with content, peers, and professors. Members of the learning community undergo a process of social apprenticeship in which they benefit from both peer and facilitator support and guidance within activities directed towards course outcomes.

Based upon survey results from a recent ATS conference on spiritual formation online, Tait argued that traditional course content cannot simply be transferred to the internet without significant changes to methods of presentation and learning activities. The change is based upon interaction, and students and professors must be committed to making the interaction work. Online environments can help students to engage in learning in life changing ways; however, it can—if the teaching is also left to the computer—leave them feeling that they are enrolled in a correspondence course. In addition, collaboration does not necessarily result in productive activity and learning if totally free and unguided (Lakkala, 2007). If designed and used effectively, student-centered online learning can encourage and motivate students to become involved in communicating to an audience of peers, rather than composing assignments only for the professor (Berge and Collins, 1995).

Online learning incorporates the philosophy and methodology of experiential education, promoting inquiring forms of learning that engage learners in the experiences through engaged, student-centered process driven by the situation with the online instructor serving as the expert course guide. In a survey of over 189,000 randomly sampled first year and senior students in the US, Chen (2008) showed that engagement is positively related to a broad range of outcomes, most notably higher grades, student satisfaction, and persistence—all outcomes that we want to encourage in education. Our goal in this online environment is to deliver an educational setting based upon emergent, collaborative processes and student-directed inquiry, and to foster the capacity to build and sustain online learning communities by encouraging engagement through interaction, learning conversations, and reflection as part of individual and collective knowledge building.

The Online Course

Consider for a moment how you spend your time with a class-based course. You probably have used a textbook or primary resources that provided core concepts. You assume that students read this since they are accountable for it. You enriched this by preparing and delivering lectures or other presentations. You manage some kind of classroom or seminar discussions and use assessment activities that are designed to encourage students to build their knowledge and apply their insights. You hold regular office hours for personal contact with students, and of course, you grade. So in a face-to-face course, how much time do you spend?

In online learning, the same time commitment remains constant, but there are a few differences in the activities. The core curriculum presentation has become explicit and externalized. The difference between one presentation of a course and the next is based upon the variable of the student population, rather than the actual content or assignments. Developers create sequential curriculum that can apply across many groups or sections taking the same course. The job of the developers is to create those parts that will not change from one semester to the next.

The job of the instructors, or learning facilitators, is to deal with the interactive parts that change—individuals, discussions, seminars, and assignments. Since the instructor is no longer delivering content, the time usually spent in on-ground classes preparing and delivering presentations becomes devoted to the actual progress of individuals, groups, or the class as a whole. Activities such as grading and office hours remain fairly constant, except that they are delivered through the written word rather than the spoken word.

Consider the trade-off in time. There is no content preparation or delivery since these already exist in a well-designed course. These are isolated, content-rich activities, generally created by a subject expert. Other activities focus on the student variables, as a group and as individuals. This is where the creativity of the facilitator is important. In the online environment, the time that would be spent in isolated activity can now be attentive to student learning. As a result of this time flexibility, a facilitator should plan to include 15-20% of the total lecture notes of a course with a higher frequency at the early stages.

Designers focus on didactic content and sequencing, while instructors focus on activities of individuals and groups. We want to ensure that all students have what they need and know what to do with it in order to interact and contribute successfully to the class learning process.

Seven Principles of Good Teaching Practice in the Classroom

In response to the question of improving post-secondary education, Chickering and Gamson (1987) articulated seven best practices in post-secondary teaching. These principles have been widely accepted as defining the best practices for effective, class-based teaching in post-secondary and post-graduate classes. Faculty are generally comfortable with classroom teaching and its attendant activities and can identify how they are already incorporating these seven principles.

1. **Good practice encourages contact between students and faculty.**

   Frequent student-faculty contact in and out of classes is the most important factor in student motivation and involvement. Faculty concern helps students get through rough times and keep on working. Knowing a few faculty members well enhances students' intellectual commitment and encourages them to think about their own values and future plans.

2. **Good practice develops reciprocity and cooperation among students.**

   Learning is enhanced when it is more like a team effort than a solo race. Good learning, like good work, is collaborative and social, not competitive and isolated. Working with others often increases involvement in learning. Sharing one's own ideas and responding to others' reactions sharpens thinking and deepens understanding.

3. **Good practice encourages active learning.**

   Learning is not a spectator sport. Students do not learn much just by sitting in classes listening to teachers and spitting out answers. They must talk about what they are learning, write about it, relate it to past experiences and apply it to their daily lives. They must make what they learn part of themselves.

4. Good practice gives prompt feedback.

Students need appropriate feedback on performance in order to benefit from courses. When getting started, students need help in assessing existing knowledge and competence. In classes, students need frequent opportunities to perform and receive suggestions for improvement. At various points, both during classes and at the end, students need chances to reflect on what they have learned, what they still need to know, and how to self-assess.

5. Good practice emphasizes time on task.

Time plus energy equals learning. There is no substitute for time on task. Learning to use one's time well is critical for students and professionals alike. Students need help in learning effective time management. Allocating realistic amounts of time means effective learning for students and effective teaching for faculty. How an institution defines time expectations for students, faculty, administrators, and other professional staff can establish the basis of high performance for all.

6. Good practice communicates high expectations.

Expect more and you will get more. High expectations are important for everyone—for the poorly prepared, for those unwilling to exert themselves, and for the bright and well-motivated. Expecting students to perform well becomes a self-fulfilling prophecy when teachers hold high expectations for themselves and make extra efforts.

7. Good practice respects diverse talents and ways of learning.

There are many roads to learning. People bring different talents and styles of learning to our institution. Brilliant students in the seminar room may be weaker in written work. Students rich in hands-on experience may not do so well with theory. Students need the opportunity to show their talents and learn in ways that work for them. Then they can be pushed to learn in new ways that do not come so easily.

An engaged student is a learning student. The application of these principles supports the student-centred learning approach by encouraging student engagement. And this is our goal as educators.

Best Practices in Online Teaching

Chickering and Gamson's principles are based upon traditional model of teaching, but they apply equally in the online environment (Chickering and Ehrmann, 1996), although their application can be somewhat different. This section will apply the seven principles to the online teaching environment and suggest specific teaching tactics for implementing them.

1. Encourage student-faculty contact and interaction.

Just as frequent student-faculty contact is a key factor in student motivation, intellectual commitment, and personal development, faculty contact is a critical factor in online student success and satisfaction. Students need explicit guidelines for communication. In online learning, meeting this first principle of good practice is easily accomplished by four simple measures.

1. Make sure that instructor contact information is clearly delineated within the course site.
2. Stipulate and maintain timelines for responses to email communications. A statement such as "All emails with be responded to within 12 hours" on your contact information page and your syllabus lets students know that you will not be at your computer 24 hours a day, and it sets a reasonable expectation for a response. It also establishes a point at which students should resend communication in case there has been a digital glitch.
3. Convey instructions on where various types of communication should be directed. For example, "Email questions about any software or hardware problems to tech support not the instructor," or "The main discussion forum is for questions or comments that are of interest to the whole class; concerns about specific exam questions or your grade should be directed to me privately via email."
4. Know how to reach your students in a timely manner if concerns arise. You may consider asking for a "Student

Information Sheet" with email addresses, phone numbers, employer and work hours. This document provides you with various methods of contacting students. If a complex question arises, verbal conversations are sometimes more productive than repeated email messages.

Some Teaching Tactics:

- Offer multiple forms of contact, including emails, phone calls, face-to-face, online chats.
- Establish virtual office hours: times when the students know you are available for online chats, phone calls, or email.
- Acknowledge initial receipt of students' email with an automatic email reply.
- Differentiate types of inquiries and your response time (receipt of message, personal question, content question, procedural question, assignment feedback). Not every message is of equal importance or will require equal time for your response.
- Inform students that infrastructure problems (server, etc.) are beyond your control and may occasionally impact response time.
- Use forums to create an online learning community.
    - Share your personal biographical sketch with students.
    - Make an effort to find out basic information about your students.
    - Try to introduce students to each other.
    - Refer to your students by their first names.

2. Encourage student cooperation.

Learning is enhanced through a cooperative approach, characterized by positive interdependence, interaction, personal responsibility, collaborative skills, and group processing. Much of this is achieved through discussion forum interaction.

Since asynchronous discussion forum activities can transition a group of students from "virtual" strangers into a cohesive learning community, well-constructed discussion assignments, generally created in advance by the course developer, and balanced instructor participation encourage and require student cooperation. In the classroom, the professor is often the central focus of discussions, but in online learning, in order to promote students' social connectedness and the free exchange of ideas, instructors must become a discussion facilitator rather than the leader. Instructor discussion forum tasks include establishing the topic, monitoring participation, promoting collaboration or redirection, prompting student clarification of errors, and summarizing threads or discussions.

Just a word of caution, though: When instructors interject their views on the discussion board, the conversation often ceases since students will often perceive this position as the "true" or "correct" answer. Facilitation rather than conversation or written lecturing is the preferred instructor's role in forums. Informed, open-ended questioning entries that can include comments or summaries and that redirect the discussion can be a useful tactic.

Some Teaching Tactics:

- Create assignments that require students to respond to peers' work/assignments.
- Use techniques for fostering student cooperation:
  - Peer reviews
  - Discussion forums
  - Group projects
  - Student groups
  - Team learning
  - Peer grading, based upon rubric specifications. Justify the grades that you assign.
- Avoid definitive responses in discussion forums. These will often shut down any further interaction.
- Use open-ended questioning with any appropriate prefatory remarks to redirect and restimulate the collaborative exploration.

For the first discussion assignment, an "ice-breaker" question helps students become comfortable with their virtual classmates. This is usually created as part of course development A task requiring learners to introduce themselves to the class, explain why they are taking the course, and identify two things they hope to learn by the end of the semester is a low stakes conversation that encourages student engagement. You should respond to pretty well every one of these "ice-breaker" lectures. Subsequent discussion exercises should will focus on a central concept or topic covered in the course material, and your load is less onerous.

3. Encourage active learning.

To maximize learning, students must interact with the material they are learning, write about it, relate it to past experiences, and incorporate what they are learning into their worldview.

Students should participate in a variety of engaging assignments. Learner-centered course design, typical for collaborative online courses, requires that students do more than simply read, write, and respond. Active learning activities are needed to foster virtual student engagement. Online learning can be ideal for varied pedagogies and innovative active learning activities. Small group activities, seminars, and papers, for example, are challenging and provide evidence of student learning, and are easily constructed. Case studies or personal application are also effective methods method for motivating and engaging learners.

Some Teaching Tactics:

- Encourage student questions, input, and feedback; clearly state that all points of view are welcome and respected.
- Follow up on students who are lagging or not participating.
- Ask students to provide and critique URLs that relate to the class and can enrich learning.
- Ask students to teach their forum group or for the group to teach the rest of the class.
- Ask student to develop/create learning activities and projects.

- Ask students to critique other students' work and allow the opportunity to revise assignments based upon the peer feedback.
- Ask students to reflect on their performance, their progress, their problems, and their process. What have you learned (in your own words)? Why is this new knowledge important?
- Pose discussion questions that foster critical thinking, problem solving, and extended and wide-ranging dialog. Preset discussion questions are designed to encourage divergent thinking, collaboration, and convergence. Your role is to encourage collaboration and convergence in your learners' thinking.
- Use quizzes/questions that require students to review the content (self-check or automatically graded online).
- Follow up reading assignments with discussions, simulations, or applications to cases and student, personal experiences.
- Offer frequent short assignments/quizzes or other frequent "in progress" feedback opportunities.
- Establish replies and responses as important values of online discussions through tone, modeling, and grade weighting.

4. Give prompt feedback.

The instructor role is key as it gives the students help in assessing their knowledge and competence. Students need ongoing feedback along with formative and summative assessment comments.

Formative assessment is a classroom tool designed to provide students with feedback about their learning prior to conducting any graded evaluations. The purpose of formative assessment is to improve student learning and allow students to practice self-assessment and thus these types of activities are almost always ungraded. Summative assessments are graded activities evaluating student mastery of particular learning objectives.

Much of the activity of a facilitator involves formative evaluation, presented both within the discussion forums and through private email. Formative evaluation is used within forums to support discussions and to introduce other avenues of inquiry. In the discussion forums, formative evaluation often takes the form of discussion summarization, assessment, and direction to the group as a whole. Facilitators draw discussion threads together, encapsulating them, and refocusing the direction of the discussion, generally through the use of open-ended questions. Email and system messaging is a multi-purpose tool for personal feedback, encouragement, and direction for individual students.

Providing students prompt feedback on summative assessments is also important. Evaluation rubrics posted in every course help with this. Rubrics are intended to make expectations explicit, quantifiable, easily matched to assignment characteristics, and directly related to observable and measurable outcomes. Explicit rubrics set forth precise criteria and instructors can show students exactly how work is being evaluated. These simplify the summative evaluation process by communicating detailed explanations of what constitutes excellence for a given task, allowing the facilitator to focus instead on more qualitative and personal feedback.

Some Teaching Tactics:

- Respond with frequent email or discussion board comments: with answers to questions, comments about lesson/unit content, giving directions and additional information.
- Return tests, papers, assignments within 7-10 days.
- Hold virtual office hours for students to discuss their graded work.
- Post or sends grades regularly.
- Acknowledge all student questions.
- Use quizzes/questions that require students to review the content (credit-based tests that are automatically graded online, or self-checking exercises)
- Use grading rubrics to evaluate clearly and consistently student work.
- Post outstanding student work, and explain what makes it good.
- Provide annotated models of assignments, such as a model student essay or journal entry, to demonstrate expectations.
- Follow up on feedback via email or phone if students do not respond initially to feedback.

5. **Emphasize time on task.**

Learning takes place when time is used effectively and actively. Students often associate online courses with a self-paced, independent study learning environment; and many select online courses because they need flexible timelines to balance busy schedules with educational obligations. But online courses need deadlines and defined expectations. For asynchronous education to promote deep, meta-cognitive learning rather than surface memorization of information, students need time to evaluate, challenge, and make meaning of course materials. This reflective process is essential for higher-order thinking and is a pedagogically designed characteristic of collaborative, online courses. Clear guidelines and regular expectations encourage learners to spend time on task, they help them to mediate their schedules, and they deter perpetual procrastination.

An equilibrium between unrestricted timelines and rigid due dates can be achieved by adopting ranged deadlines. Facilities within learning management systems allow faculty to set ranges for assignments—drop boxes can be opened and closed at different times, or times tests can take place throughout a specified period.

Some Teaching Tactics:

- Clearly define and explain course goals, performance objectives, grading and evaluation criteria, and grading rubrics.
- Indicate the relative emphasis on facts, critical thinking, analysis, reasoning, etc.
- Establish and enforce deadlines for assignments.
- Let students know much time it will take to do the assignments.
- Outline the steps in completing each of the assignments. Break the assignment into smaller, more manageable parts if appropriate.

- Use quizzes/questions that require students to review the content (self-check or automatically graded online).
- Build in a rewards system of points for all student work.
- Try and include a weekend day to accommodate students who work regular Monday through Friday schedules.

6. Communicate high and consistent expectations.

When faculty set high but attainable goals, academic achievement increases. Goals are stated in the learning outcomes in the course syllabus and supported by the grading rubrics, but these are the 'ground-rules' level. Faculty interaction with students—both within forums and intended for the group and within private e-mails for the individual—should continue to encourage reflections, connections between concepts, and deeper, personal discovery.

Some Teaching Tactics:

- The course syllabus is available on a public, website, and on the course. It clearly defines and explains course goals, performance objectives, grading and evaluation criteria, grading rubrics, and indicates the relative emphasis on facts, critical thinking, analysis, and reasoning.
- Course activities address the same objectives as on-campus course activities.
- Course requirements/assignments/activities are equivalent in difficulty and depth to those in the on-campus sections of the course.

- Students are evaluated with the same emphasis and level of difficulty as the on-campus sections.
- Instructors set high standards for themselves and model through example.
- Communication—both public and private—encourages content-specific and enrichment-based explorations and reflection.

7. Respect diverse talents and ways of learning.

Attention to diversity of learning is built into a course through the instructional design process. Recognizing the learning styles of others can increase a student's repertoire of learning strategies.

Some Teaching Tactics:

- Ask students to complete a learning style assessment questionnaire at the beginning of the semester.
- Design more than one method of assessment and demonstration of student achievement. Allow students to choose from different possible modes of project presentation, established up front in an agreement between you and the student.
- Encourage students to use the Web and other resources and media to master course content by incorporating Web-based assignments or directions into the curriculum and reading assignments.

- Be sensitive to possible cultural differences, especially communicating with students for whom English is a second language.
- If possible, provide alternatives to reading text, such as audio explanations of complicated materials.

Some guidelines for online teaching

Henry and Winters (2008) argued that sound pedagogical use of the tools for learning can engage and immerse students in the learning experience. They propose a series of principles that can guide the act of teaching in online environments.

1. The online world is its own medium. It has a different dynamic than a campus course. Content has been developed and integrated before the learners arrive, and this provides a basic pathway. But there is a need to provide alternative pathways and greater depth for learners, depending upon their interests and issues. Facilitators may find that there is a constant need for elaboration and explanation.

2. "Online" is a verb. The goal is to engage purposefully and strategically the learners using tools such as discussions and other usually technically-mediated interactions such as email or telephone. The intent is to create and manage a full learning experience made up of the interaction of content, learners, and learning facilitators in which content is both available and students can actively contribute to it.

3. A great online course is defined by teaching rather than technology. If an online course is to be excellent, it depends upon excellent teaching. The technology simply provides a set of tools and related tactics to support this. Specific tactics will help to promote excellence and, in turn, lead to greater student satisfaction. These include,
    - a quick turn-around time on emails and assignments,
    - frequent and engaged contact and personal feedback,
    - good communication skills, and
    - an ability be real and genuine, spontaneity in technically-mediated communication.

4. A strong social presence is essential. As a simple definition, social presence is the degree to which a person is perceived as a real person, rather than just the author of a few static postings. Community enables deeper learning through sustained communication aimed at the construction of meaning, and it takes effort to build this, especially at the beginning of a course when students are beginning to feel out expectations of themselves and others. It also takes effort to sustain it. Using tools such as collaborative learning, introductory discussion forums, enhanced communication, humour, and small group activities can help.

5. Be ready to adopt multiple levels of expertise. Faculty members often find themselves in multiple roles: subject matter expert, discussion and community facilitator, and even learning process expert. For most institutions, there is a technical support group available to help problem solve, but you are still the front line and may receive questions before the support group.

6. <u>Little things can make a big difference.</u> Any extras that you can do to help students achieve the levels specified in the course rubrics is worth doing. Your facilitation role is to help students to achieve these. Some tactics that you might try include:

- Providing exemplars of course assignments. These can be used to model an appropriate response to an assignment and reduce anxiety.
- Providing direction, both to the group and to individuals, on how to be a self-guided learner; for example, what does the model self-guided learner do in order to produce a 200 word reflection? Are there effective strategies for studying for a test? What is the most effective way to manage and communicate within a group project?
- Using brief, personal emails. These can be as simple as, "I got your assignment. Thanks. I'll be looking at it in the next few days." Or "Hi John, You might want to think about this idea for your discussion entries. Mary, in particular, might be interested." These are quick, toss-off emails, but they keep the contact and the personal touch alive.

Some General Tactics for Online Educators

1. Have a clear purpose. Without this, there is no obvious direction.
2. Get personal. Make your course a personal experience as soon as students log in. Create the sense of community by incorporating such things as pictures, biographies, ice-breakers. Encourage students to do the same.

3. Know your learners. Be familiar with them as people, not just names. What do they hope to achieve?

4. Know your tools. You are the expert and role model, so you will need to communicate effectively using the tools available. Know how to use things like:

    a. Email
    b. Forums
    c. Chats or office hours

5. Communicate clearly using language that learners will understand. We are an academic institution, but think about the tone and language that you use in a classroom or seminar. You want to capture this and talk through your fingers to real people.

6. Create an environment that supports both a warm and fuzzy community feeling and productive collaboration. Most learners come to your course with personal motives, seeking skills and experiences that they can use for personal reasons. Moments of connection with peers will help to support this.

7. Like your students. This allows you to make a more significant difference because you see them as individuals with hopes and dreams. This helps to motivate you and learners through any difficulties.

8. Lead by example. You are the model of scholar and teacher. Much of what you will communicate is tacit knowledge. You need to model best practices.

9. Respond thoughtfully to feedback. Sometimes participants want to know that they have been noticed by the facilitator.

10. Value learner contributions: A community of learners becomes effective when participants start to contribute willingly to discussions, and even more when they can initiate and peer-facilitate these.

11. Use enabling questions to open or revitalize online interaction. Learners need to find their own answers. Hold back a bit with answers and use questioning that deepens the conversation or provokes a shift of phase. Support effective leadership within the learning community. In later stages of courses, most action should come from the students. This includes leadership by participants. Allow and encourage them operate more.

12. Be a facilitator, not a dictator. Give students the freedom to drive discussions. As a 'guide on the side' your role is to facilitate rather than control discussions.

Conclusion

A great course is a function of great teaching and student engagement. Your role, as facilitator, is critical in order to make this happen. Communication, both responsive and proactive, is the key.

Enjoy the course. The teaching experience online is different from the on-ground experience because you have direct inspection of and influence on both the group and individual student experience and success. It is a more personal and interpersonal experience since your goal is to help a group made up of unique individuals learn together and engage in a personal quest for truth. A facilitator is an enabler of this student-centred learning.

References

Berge, Z. L., and Collins, M. (1995). Introduction to computer-mediated communication and the online classroom in higher education. In Z. L. Berge and M. Collins (eds.) *Computer mediated communication and the online classroom,*Vol. 2: Higher education. Cresskill: Hampton Press Inc..

** Chen, Pu-Shi Daniel, Gonyea, Robert, and Kuh, George (2008). *Learning at a distance: Engaged or not. Innovate.*

Chickering, Arthur, and Ehrmann, Stephen C (Oct., 1996). Implementing the seven principles: Technology as lever. *AAHE Bulletin*, 3-6.

Chickering and Gamson (Mar., 1987) . Seven principles for good practice in undergraduate education. *The American Association for Higher Education Bulletin.* Available: http://honolulu.hawaii.edu/intranet/committees/FacDevCom/gui debk/teachtip/7princip.htm

Forman, E.A., and Cazden, C. B. (1985). Exploring Vygotskian perspectives in education: The value of peer interaction. In J. V. Wertsch (Ed.) *Culture, communication, and cognition.* New York: Cambridge University Press.

Henry, Jim, and Meadows, Jeff (Winter, 2008). An absolutely riveting online course: Nine principles for excellence in web-based teaching. *Canadian Journal of Learning and technology* V34(1) Winter.

Lakkala, M. (n.d.). The pedagogical design of technology enhanced collaborative learning. Fe-ConE – Framework for e-learning contents evaluation project: A position paper. Centre for research on networked learning and knowledge building. Available https://www.researchgate.net/publication/241900666_The_pedag ogical_design_of_technology_enhanced_collaborative_learning Accessed June 2007.

Scardamalia, M. and Bereiter, C. (2003) Knowledge building. In *Encyclopedia of Education* (2nd ed.) New York: Macmillan Reference, 1370-1373.

Tait, Jennifer Woodruff (2010). Time for reflection: High quality online education requires careful thought and ample resources. *In Trust Magazine* Vol. 21, No.2. New Year. 10-12.

Vygotsky, L. S. (1978) *Mind in society: The development of higher psychological processes.* Cambridge MA: Harvard University Press.

Wertsch, J. V. (1985). *Vygotsky and the social formation of mind.* Cambridge, MA. Harvard University Press.

10

eQuity: Considering "Otherness" in the Online Classroom

Timothy Paul Westbrook

Do you remember what it was like? In just a short few weeks schools around the world quickly made the decision out of desperation during a global pandemic to move from face-to-face meetings to some version of education online. The question of whether it should be done became a matter of how to do it and how to make the transition quickly. For better or for worse, I suppose that every employed academician and every enrolled student now in the age of COVID-19 has some experience with online education.

This book you're reading serves as useful guide for the general masses of educators who are retooling in order to be the educators they imagined themselves to be in spite of separation of space and time. Written by experts in the discipline of distance education, the book offers a combination of principles for practice as well as empirical research to assist in policy making and preparation for what might lie ahead. However, there is a concern that overarches all of the principles and practices of teaching and learning. It is a question that ought to be at the forefront of all faith-based education, whether online or face-to-face, that is, how do we create learning spaces that give equitable opportunities for learning, especially when we have a diverse population of learners?

Larry Hopperton (Ch. 7, 159-166) in his chapter on accessibility addresses the various aspects of physical and learning challenges that ought to be considered when designing an online course. While some may consider accessibility a matter of compliance, it is more a matter of moral obligation. Any course designed for one should be accessible to all, and faith-based institutions have an opportunity to lead the way in how to design, create, and implement learning experiences that provide equitable and safe spaces.

In addition, matters of race ought to be considered when it comes to the online classroom. W. E. B. Du Bois eloquently described the "double consciousness" experienced by black citizens at the turn of the twentieth century in his book *The Souls of Black Folk*: "It is a peculiar sensation, this double-consciousness, this sense of always looking at one's self through the eyes of others" (Du Bois and Huggins, 1986, 364). Du Bois represented a desire to be accepted as fully American and fully black. He envisioned a world that would move beyond racial divisions through mutual learning and partnership. Du Bois's vision was progressive and continues to inspire scholars today (Brookfield, 2005, 279; hooks, 2003, 3; Ladson-Billings and Tate IV, 2006, 14; Outlaw, 1996, 5; West, 2001, 11).

A question for faith-based based institutions now in the twenty-first century would be whether education has moved beyond the double-consciousness phenomenon for underrepresented students. The spring of 2020 brought to international attention the tragic deaths of Ahmaud Arbery, Breonna Taylor, and George Floyd. The outcry in the streets and the powerful impact of Black Lives Matter, after years of building to this moment, suggest that Du Bois's vision has not yet been accomplished in U.S. American society; so this might suggest that in online spaces justice is still being sought. Indeed, problems of race and the internet are as complex as the dimensions of culture and society that create social problems in the first place (Nakamura and Chow-White, 2012).

When it comes to racism and social justice, this is a tough issue to address adequately, especially given that discrimination is a global phenomenon with the specific issues varying from region to region and country to country (De Vos, 2006). For the sake of this chapter, the question may be asked in this way, "In what ways, if any, does race matter in online education?" The short answer is that online spaces are sociological spaces like any other, which means matters of race do play into the experience.

The age of COVID-19 has also exposed the international connectivity of online education in ways that may have escaped the attention of location-centered institutions. For example, many institutions of higher education in the United States have students "stranded" in their home countries who are forced to participate in classes remotely simply because of travel restrictions or because of the uncertainty of being granted visas. Schools who want to keep their students have found ways to offer their courses online. In the meantime, the international community is fully engaged with online solutions to education. Though I am writing from a U.S. American perspective, I have visited with acquaintances in Europe, Asia, and Africa; and each situation is different. Around the world educators are creatively finding solutions to the pandemic with varying degrees of online and remote learning. We see into this new age more opportunities to connect with global academic networks. While people have "sheltered in place," over online media, the world has gotten a little smaller, and skills for online communication have become daily necessities. Yet, if the world is getting closer on the internet, there is still the matter of intercultural expectations for "normal" that have to be navigated in the academic spaces in order to maximize the benefits of multiplicity in the classroom rather than be subjected to barriers that frustrate progress, learning, and success.

The purpose of this chapter is to explore from a faith-based perspective how online classrooms may account for "Otherness" in such a way that creates safe spaces for student learning and personal growth. I first present a brief vignette to illustrate the intersection of race, gender, and national culture. Second, I summarize major themes regarding matters of culture and race online. Third, I offer a model for systemic accountability that helps institutions be intentional about student success for students who may be faced with sociologically driven challenges. Given that most of my experience and research has focused on higher education, I center the chapter on the post-secondary student experience and what colleges and universities may do in order to offer academic learning environments that account for diversity and attend to the variety of perspectives students bring to the online classroom. For some, diversity is a challenge, but for the astute and culturally sensitive academician, diversity is a rich resource that enhances the overall experience for all who share in the variegated educational tapestry.

Dorothy Goes to College:
A Short Story of Culture, Race, and Gender

Consider the young lady, named Dorothy, who has grown up in a small village not too far from Lusaka, the capital city of Zambia. Dorothy was smart and a hard worker. While she always helped out with her at-home responsibilities, she also was a diligent student at her village school. She always earned high marks. Her teachers, her parents, and her extended family hoped that Dorothy would be able to attend the university and make something special with her life. Dorothy felt indebted to her community for the encouragement she had received all of her life. No matter what doors were to open to her in the future, she always had in mind that she wanted to be a blessing to her family and to her village.

One day she was talking with a preacher who was visiting from Lusaka, and he mentioned how there was a university in America that was offering an online degree in theology. If accepted, Dorothy would be able to attend this university with all of her U.S. expenses paid for by a special scholarship. Her only costs would be the price of a dependable computer and connection to the internet. Dorothy was surprised that this preacher was suggesting a degree in theology given that in her tradition it is nearly unheard of for women to be trained in pastoral ministry. However, the idea intrigued her. The more she thought about it, the more excited she got about the idea of earning an American university degree. The fact that the degree was in theology only intrigued her more because as a religious person herself, she thought that perhaps God was doing more with her life than she expected of herself.

When Dorothy's parents heard about this opportunity, they got excited about it as well. They told their friends and extended family, who then gathered together to try to find a way for Dorothy to pursue her degree online. While she would be saving $80,000 (US currency) of tuition because of the scholarship, a price tag unfathomable by Dorothy's parents, the cost of a good computer and reliable internet would not come easy. But because of the faith that Dorothy's community had in her, several people worked together to make sure she had the device and the access she needed for her online school. Dorothy felt great honor by the trust and respect she received from her family and community. With so much support, she was determined not to disappoint anyone.

The next challenge came as soon as Dorothy tried to apply for the university. She received an email from the university that had several links that led to several webpages and forms. Dorothy was not used to filling out online forms. In fact, her cultural background was what some might consider to be high context (see Hall, 1976), which means that most of the time in her context information and decisions were made through relationships, conversation, and sometimes through collaborative efforts. The online forms were confusing. She invited others to help her sort through the forms, and although she eventually submitted her application online, it was with great effort and frustration. Little did Dorothy realize, nor did her university realize, the admissions process of forms, emails, and links were culturally bound within expectations of a low-context culture in which communication relies on direct, verbal expressions, whether written or spoken, and less on community driven understandings of how things should be.

In addition to the application, Dorothy was told she had to submit something called a "transcript" from her previous schooling. Since she had also attended a vocational school in Lusaka for two years, her American university required Dorothy to have this transcript sent directly from her school in Lusaka. She understood what she had to do, but as she approached the administrative offices of her Zambian school, she had a difficult time helping them understand why she needed the transcript and why it needed to be sent directly to the school in the U.S. Things finally were resolved, but not without the expenses of multiple trips to the capital city and also additional "financial persuasions" for the transcript to be mailed.

Once Dorothy was accepted into the university, the emails from the U.S. continued with links and short messages, but from her perspective, she longed for a conversation with her professors or classmates. She wished that she could see them face-to-face. She got confused multiple times by the word-heavy syllabi her teachers gave her without any further comment. When she would ask a question, her teachers would simply reply, "Did you read the syllabus? The answer to your question is in the syllabus." She also had trouble with the time gap between her university and her own time zone. Sometimes it would take a couple of days for her to close the communication gap, even when matters were time sensitive. The occasional power outages complicated things further. Overall, she missed the learning community she was used to.

Not only did she have to overcome the challenges of being enculturated into a new educational system, she noticed that there were some in her classes online who were openly talking negatively about "foreigners." Some of her professors appeared to be critical of her writing because of her Zambianisms. She even noticed that some of her white classmates avoided working with her in group projects or when they did work together, the white U.S. students dominated the conversations and took charge without asking for her help. To make matters worse, the further she advanced in her theology degree, the more suspicion she experienced from her community at home who wondered if she was allowing "progressive" Western theology taint her theological perspective. They wondered if she was going to start "usurping" male authority once she completed her degree. In spite of these challenges, Dorothy persisted. She reasoned that it was God who opened this door, and God would help her through to the end.

Reflecting on Dorothy's Situation

As we consider Dorothy's story, there are multiple issues that surface. First, Dorothy's cultural context was what the literature labels as a high-context culture, and she was applying for a university that was in a low-context culture. According to Hall's (1976, 91–101) classic categories, in high-context cultures communication is more relationship oriented and non-verbal. Conversations may be exchanged through mere glances or non-verbal cues. Expectations for roles remain static and often are directed for the good of the whole of the community and not the individuals. In the low-context culture, communication is verbal and occurs explicitly. Non-verbal cues are either missed or ignored. Individual goals have a better chance of being advanced without necessarily being in alignment with the goals of the community. Whereas high-context and collectivism tend to be paired, low-context and individualism tend to co-exist culturally (see (De Vos, 2006). Because Dorothy's default was high context, she found it difficult to navigate the low-context system of her American university. She was able to solve her own problems, but not without trouble. It was unlikely that the Admissions office in the U.S. had any idea how difficult it was for her to overcome these cultural differences.

Second, once Dorothy started taking classes, she was one international student among many U.S. American students. She had never been in a minority situation before. She had never had to experience her own identity as an international student or as a "foreigner." The negative comments from her classmates caught her by surprise, and it damaged her emotionally. In a similar way, she had never thought of herself as racially underrepresented. All of her classmates to this point were from the same location and had the same social experiences. She had only had black Zambian classmates. While she had heard about racial discrimination in other regions, she had not experienced it herself. These moments were confusing and disturbing. They made her question whether she had made the right choice by enrolling in this degree program.

Third, although Dorothy's community had initially rallied behind her to help her get her degree, she was confused by how it seemed that the local pastoral leadership was dismissing her education and even treating her like a rival. Dorothy was aware of the cultural restrictions on women in her church community, and she had no intentions to disrupt the status quo as far as this was concerned. But the reaction of the men in her church community hurt her greatly. She internalized her pain and questioned her own motives. Now that she was an "educated woman" in ministry, she wondered if she was somehow bringing shame to her parents, her family, and her church.

While the details of Dorothy's story are fiction, the experiences shared in this vignette are based on multiple conversations with international students as well as research (see Nanton, 2005; Sweeting and Westbrook, 2021). Dorothy experienced the trauma of what happens when an academic institution is not prepared to provide safe learning environments when there is an intersectionality of race, culture, and gender. Her situation may not represent everyone who faces one or more of these sources for discrimination, but her case serves as an appropriate image for us to consider as we think about Otherness in the online classroom. Each person in an online class has a story. The more attentive to the variety of stories we may have in our learning communities, the better we will be able to generate an atmosphere of care and support in such a way that will minimize the discouragement and lead toward success.

Freedom v. Extension of Racism in Online Education

Online education is a global phenomenon, and scholarship has not ignored the need to learn more about how social dynamics may manifest or need to be managed in distance education (for a more detailed exploration culture and online education see (Toprak and Kumtepe, 2018; Westbrook, 2014). Research has presented a blend of both positive and negative experiences with online education from the perspective of culture and race. Major themes may be broadly grouped into two: the wall of anonymity and the wall of separation.[1]

---

[1] Some of this information is being adapted from my blog post entitled "eQuality: Race and Online Education" on the Wabash Center for Teaching and Learning website at the following url:

The Wall of Anonymity as Freedom

The faceless nature of online education for some people actually creates a sense of liberation from cultural barriers that typically might restrict. One respondent in a recent study I conducted described the online interface as "the wall" that protected students, in her case as an African American in a predominantly white school, from "racial disparities" (Westbrook, 2017, 118). Al-Harthi (2005, 7), described the layer of protection afforded by online learning as giving an "impression of anonymity," especially if the course is primarily written-based.

When one becomes self-conscious of being located in a minority position then that could result in concerns of safety and stereotype threat that often results in students' underachieving due to the added stress they feel as an underrepresented person (Steele, 2009; Verschelden, 2017). However, some have reported that being online reduces fears. Multiple students in my interviews about African American experiences on predominantly white campuses shared how they felt protected online. One person said he was less worried about stereotyping given that no one knew what he looked like (Westbrook, 2017, 118).

In a similar way, Ibarra (2000, 7), while researching Latina doctoral students who were Puerto Rican, Mexican-American, and from the Caribbean, noted how the written-based courses protected his interviewees from prejudice based on dialect. As one of his interviewees said, "No one can hear my accent on the keyboard."

---

https://www.wabashcenter.wabash.edu/2019/05/equality-race-and-online-education/.

When describing cultural variables in an online course that had students predominantly from the Arab Gulf, Al-Harthi (2005) noted how gender bias was reduced in that both women and men felt free to interact in the course. In addition, one of his interviewees reported that she did not feel threatened by anti-Muslim tendencies because her classmates could not see her *hijab*.

In sum, when a person is interacting in an online course from her or his own context, the student is approaching the learning activities from a comfortable and personally selected environment. The extra layer of a digital screen or written-based communication for some people reduces fear over discrimination and anxiety from stereotype threat (the internalization of stereotypes that results in underachievement). Recognizing how the digital "wall" can in some cases reduce stress and give open access to course materials and encourage interaction is a key advantage for course designers and teachers. Not being face-to-face may cause just enough disruption to expected social cues that allow for students to be seen for who they are and not what they look like or sound like in comparison to the instructors or others in the course.

The Wall of Separation as an Extension of Racism

While there is hope that an online course may disrupt racism and other forms of social restrictions, online courses ought not to be considered as culturally or sociologically neutral spaces. Online spaces are just like any domain in which people inhabit. Although there may be a lingering stigma with online communication that once a person enters into social media, an online course, or some other digital spaces that they leave behind their true identities for a new avatar-like replacement self, in reality every presentation of self that one loads into an online presence is in some way a representation of who he or she really is. Even something mundane like an idealistic "social media self" is not dissimilar to how one might dress according to certain styles in order to send a message of how they want others to perceive them. The good nature of humanity can be seen online as well as the pitfalls of a society corrupted by sin and evil. Matters of prejudice and racism do exist in online courses, and it is the role of the educator to identify the problems and to manage them.

First, people may choose online spaces based on racialization. About ten years ago, Danah Boyd (2012) interviewed teenage students about their preferences of MySpace or Facebook. What she found was that there tended to be a "white flight" from MySpace to Facebook. One of her respondents said, "It's not really racist, but I guess you could say that. I'm not really into racism, but I think that MySpace now is more like ghetto or whatever" (262). The students in Boyd's study reported this migration for racist reasons, whether or not they admitted that was the reason behind it. As Boyd concluded, "Teen preference for MySpace or Facebook went beyond simple consumer choice; it reflected a reproduction of social categories that exist in schools throughout the United States…. The choice between MySpace and Facebook became racialized" (262).

Even though in the early 2020s social media culture has been quick to identify racists and "cancel" celebrities and institutions where racism and bigotry might be detected, even this reaction against racism online is an extension of a cultural frustration. In the meantime, new social media emerge, such as MeWe, as alternatives to Facebook in 2020 and 2021. Anecdotally, the reasons for migrating from Facebook sound quite similar to the reasons given in Boyd's research. If we know that racist social phenomena are occurring in social media, then it is safe for us also to recognize that similar biases likely exist in our online classrooms. As educators online, we must not be over idealistic or naïve about the "permanence of racism" or *racial realism* and its impact on our digital educational spaces (Bell, Jr., 1995).

Second, racially underrepresented students are racially conscious even if the institution is not. In Ibarra's study, respondents complained about being targeted with euphemisms. They said, "If we're talking about Medicaid and about lower income people in Texas, obviously they mean Latinos or African-Americans. I guess the hardest problem I had was 'they' always talked about 'those people,' as if they didn't have an identity" (Ibarra, 2000, 14). Within their class discussions, contextually speaking, the participants in Ibarra's study felt like the "us-them" terminology were made against racial groups, even if they were encoded with other labels.

Some students I interviewed in a study of African American experiences at predominantly white institutions also shared how they were race conscious even in their online classes. One of the participants described what she noted to be "Caucasian writing." While she also emphasized that the students were not writing anything negative or racist, the fact that the interviewee recognized a difference in race through writing indicated that she was thinking about race while participating in class (Westbrook, 2017, 118). The question could be asked of the white students in her class if they, too, were equally race conscious as they participated in the class or was being white just "normal." Another respondent noted what she perceived as *white privilege* in her discussion threads. For her, the white privilege came in the form of how many of her classmates talked about how much they traveled (Westbrook, 2017, 119). Certainly, there was nothing racist about traveling, nor was this respondent hurt by their comments. Simply, her point was that they had opportunities she did not consider to be normative for her or for other African American adult learners that she knew. The point is that as an underrepresented student in her predominantly white institution, her experiences of racism in the past and knowing she was in the minority raised levels of awareness and even anxiety that factored into her online experience.

When racially underrepresented students sign up for a degree program, whether the school is online or face-to-face, they bring with them to that learning experience a lifetime of having experienced racism. Whether the school is predominantly white or has racial diversity, it would be natural for concerns of being stereotyped or discriminated against to be factored into students' overall experiences and expectations. Stereotype threat, anxiety, and insecurities are all real and documented challenges that people face when race plays a factor in academics. Although the online option may create some space and freedom from sociological barriers in education, social concerns do surface even in an online classroom, and it is up to educators to be sensitive, socially aware, and racially conscious.

Breaking the Cycle Model: A Systemic Strategy for Success

In 2015, I completed a qualitative study of 24 African American adult learners who were in non-traditional adult degree completion programs at 3 predominantly white faith-based universities. This study was published by Routledge in 2017 under the title *Spirituality,*

Community, and Race Consciousness in Adult Higher Education, and it has been the source for some of my data in this chapter (Westbrook, 2017). All 24 students shared from their lived experiences from each stage of the journey: deciding to return to school, balancing family, work, and studies while in school, and completing their degrees successfully. Their interviews were analyzed from the lens of theological anthropology and Critical Race Theory. What came out of this study was a model that I like to call the "Breaking the Cycle Model." The phrase "Breaking the Cycle" was an *in vivo* expression used by one of the interviewees concerning how his decision to earn a college degree was to help him "break the cycle" and experience some sort of socio-economic uplift (Westbrook, 2017, 76). This phrase was not only appropriate for him, but after having reflected on the major themes that emerged from the study, it became clear that individuals I interviewed were sharing with me the elements of their successful completion. Indeed, "breaking the cycle" became the apropos way of describing the phenomenon of how these students had success. It also occurred to me that astute institutions that wish to help their students complete their degrees could tap into this model as a framework for the institution.

The model consists of five themes that describe the students' journeys. The first theme is *goals* or "goals for education." No one chose to return to school with the expense and the hassle simply for one's own entertainment. The students had goals. They wanted better jobs. They wanted to advance in their careers. They wanted to be examples for their children. These goals became driving motivators that kept them focused on why they were in school again. Theme two was originally called "adult learning conditions," but I have more recently started using the single word *context*. Each student returned to school within a certain context. Usually, for the adult learner, their context included work and a family. The third theme was *support systems*, which included spouses, parents, children, friends, pastors, teachers, and staff of the institutions. We cannot overestimate the power of a support system for students, no matter what their age or life-stage may be. Theme four was *faith*. This should come as no surprise for interviews conducted at faith-based schools, but *faith* as a theme became critically important. Students' faith and the faith of their faculty and staff gave support and sustainability to students when moments of adversity would arise. Theme five was *race*. Each student had experience with racialization and those experiences for better or for worse affected their experiences at the predominantly white institutions. As I reflect on *race* in the model, it seems to me that *race* could be symbolic of any type of adversity that students face. This adversity may be any challenge, frustration, prejudice, stereotype, or even unexpected cultural gaps that work against the success of the students. They are the events that cause people to want to give up on their dreams and academic pursuits.

As I imagine this model conceptually, I see a bridge (see Figure 1). As students begin their studies they stand within their contexts with their individual responsibilities to consider, and they peer across the ravine to their goals that await them. As the students begin to walk across the bridge, they have a support system along the way. As two opposing forces, adversity tries to blow them off the bridge, or much worse, tries to destroy the bridge, while faith sustains the students and supports the bridge.

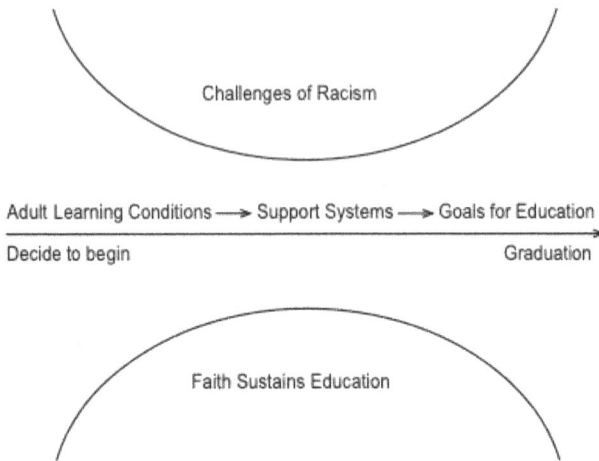

Figure 1. Breaking the Cycle Model (Westbrook, 2017, 128)

Returning to Dorothy's situation, she had all five elements. She had a context that was culturally different from her university. Her previous school experience and epistemological background, a low-context culture, her time zone, and even an honor-shame based culture comprised contextual factors. She looked forward to earning her degree, and that played a big part of what motivated her to pass through the gates of admissions. Her family and community served initially as support, but when the intersectionality of race, culture, and gender started to interfere with her self-confidence and sense of duty, what was once support turned into pressure. Finally, her faith did help. When everything else seemed to be working against her, faith gave her the strength to continue.

Now, imagine what the institution could have done differently to assist Dorothy. First, if the institution had recognized even in the admissions process that there were cultural gaps, then it would have been helpful if someone with the university could have helped enculturated Dorothy to the new system while also offering more of a high-context approach to navigating the low-context forms. Conversations online, frequent emails, phone calls, as well as visual tutorials would have made a big difference. Second, rather than belittling Dorothy for asking questions or for having a version of English that was different from the US English, the instructors should have spent time getting to know her. They should have encouraged her and provided a welcoming atmosphere. It might have also helped for the instructors to check in to see how Dorothy was coming along in her studies, ask about her family, and let her know that they supported her. Third, the teachers should have managed the classroom space with cultural sensitivity. Not everyone is trained in cultural sensitivity, but educators should have an instinct for when comments by classmates are disruptive to learning and hurtful. Not only should Dorothy's professor have challenged racist comments in the class, but he or she should have also reached out to Dorothy to reassure her that such behavior was not welcome. Fourth, the faith-based nature of the institution coupled with Dorothy's own religious convictions should have worked together as a commonality that would have given her peace even when there was adversity. Online chapel, reassuring emails from faculty and staff, and prayers offered for Dorothy would be examples of what the institution can do to connect Dorothy in a spiritual way with the faith-based mission of the school.

Online Learning as an Equitable Space for All

The "Breaking the Cycle Model" reflects how students who successfully completed their degrees navigated their academic experiences. Their success reveals to educators how the institutions might tap into these themes organizationally in order to create a degree program that provides faith-based, supportive, and safe spaces for learning. Without intentional efforts to thwart social injustices from infiltrating online communities, the same problems that trouble the physical world will also exist in the digital world. Online is not neutral, and colorblind is not an option. Digital classrooms left to unattended social processes lead to a majority wins mentality in such a way that marginalizes the underrepresented and disenfranchises those who come to their online learning programs with much sacrifice and effort. Below are some suggestions of what can be done to help our online classrooms become more equitable and attentive to the diverse needs of our students.

First, provide cultural sensitivity training for faculty and staff. Online degree programs especially need sensitivity training given that much of the communication is low-context and lacks non-verbal regulators to guide conversations. Terse messages may be received as negative. Lack of swift communication allows for students and faculty to fill in the blank space with their imaginations, and not everyone imagines positively. High power distance as well as shame-honor cultural tendencies may discourage students from asking questions. In such situations, teachers might have to pursue the students a little more in order for their international students to know it really is expected of them to ask questions. It might also help to find a mediator if the students still do not feel they are able to approach their teachers directly. Use of "us-them" terminology or expressions like "as you know" presume a homogeneous discourse community. This signals to some that if they are not part of the in-group already that they will remain on the outside.

Second, treat online spaces with the same level of care as on-ground classrooms. While we may try to convince ourselves that we treat all of our students the same, students on-ground have a homefield advantage. Students on campus can ask questions in the hallway, wait after class to approach the teacher, and address their professors "in the moment" during a class period. Students online typically are limited to written correspondence they receive from their teachers, whether that be in the form of an email, discussion, or other messaging services. We can see our students' faces on screens, but even then, it is difficult for us to detect the non-verbal nuances. Furthermore, students in a classroom on-ground do not typically have their classroom time interrupted by a knock on the door, a phone call, or emails. Online students may lose the attention of their professors to such interruptions. Organizing our online instructional time in such a way that we give our online students the attention they need will demonstrate to them that we care and that we are part of their support system. For students who may have reasons to feel insecure in the course, our attention we give them becomes hopeful reassurance.

Third, commit to eradicating racist and pejorative content and comments from the online experience. Instructional designers as well as facilitators need to be mindful of content that may be racially exclusive, ethno-centric, or misogynistic. A resource that might have been commonly used 20-30 years ago may not still connect with students in the same way. Or worse, some resources might have been produced within a cultural framework that continued to have white-supramacistic as well as paternalistic presuppositions. Course designs must be inclusive and representative of multiple points of view and experiences with the subject matter. Concerning comments from students and the teacher, great care must be given to encourage open and honest conversation in such a way that is safe for all. If a student submits a response that comes across as hateful or belittling, whether intentional or not, then it is up to the facilitator to step in an intervene. Model for the class how to deal with such comments, and contact students directly, both the one who was hurt and also the one who caused the pain.

Fourth, recognize students' contexts as resources for learning. Every student has a background. That background, whether filled with positive or negative experiences, serves as a resource for learning. As we as teachers attempt to create connections between the course content and our students' brains, the more we can help our students see how their learning is relevant to their contexts the easier it will be for these learning connections to occur. Create assignments that reflect on one's past experiences. Encourage conversations with family, friends, or church clergy and have the students report back to the rest of the class about what they learned. Not only do such interactions generate diverse discussions in the online space, but they also draw from the individual strengths that make up the mosaic of learners. In such situations, one's differing background becomes an asset to the student as well as to the overall learning community.

Fifth, show care when students face challenges in their personal lives. When students are experiencing high levels of stress in their personal lives, that stress occupies some of their cognitive space for learning. Sometimes those challenges are related to the individual. Examples may include when family members fall ill and your students need to care for them, when a student's child may be having difficulties in school and the parents need to step in and help, or if a student's employment demands more time that the student once used for studies. The emotional impact of the COVID-19 pandemic would also affect our students' personal lives. The cognitive space needed for learning competes with the stress of worrying about health and the disorientation of sheltering in place or moving from face-to-face to online learning. Teachers who show care for their students will help them find creative solutions during highly stressful situations.

Sometimes these challenges stem from more community types of issues. In the beginning of the summer of 2020 and when Black Lives Matter took to the streets in such a way that led to a nationwide and, indeed, global movement, this moment in history may be remembered as a pivotal time when awareness of institutional racism and police brutality reached main-stream consciousness. While the reality of institutional racism and police brutality have existed and victimized people of color for decades, in the summer of 2020, the voices against such injustices cried out and were heard in an interracial sort of way that will have a lasting impact on the U.S. American culture. Given the gravity of the situation, many students and faculty who connected personally with racialization were caught between the social change and their academic assignments. People in such situations need to be supported and given latitude as they take part in sociological change as well as continue their studies.

Sixth, celebrate with your students their accomplishments as they move closer to their academic goals. People like encouragement. Students like to know when they have been successful. Success can be a powerful motivator, and it is much more enjoyable than punishment. When you see international students for whom English is a second language complete a major writing assignment, praise them for their hard work. If you notice assignments are submitted in the middle of the night because your students are fitting in studying around their kids' sleep schedule, reach out and let them know you care. If you hear of some adversity through which your students have had to struggle, let your students know how you are there to help them through each step.

Seventh, of all institutions, faith-based institutions ought to be leading the way in pursuing equity in online education. Confessional commitments aside, the core question that faith-based schools tend ask is "what is good?" Faith-based schools help their students think critically about a wide variety of problems and find solutions that not only solve the problems but also address moral and ethical aspects to those problems. Racism and other forms of discrimination are moral dilemmas of the human experience that need solutions. An online school that operates from the soul to the soul, will stretch beyond measurable learning outcomes and seek to transform lives, provide uplift, and assist their students for whatever personal, social, and spiritual questions they face. Private colleges and universities will find it hard to compete with publicly funded institutions if they do not hold fast to their missions. However, those faith-based institutions that pursue fairness, equity, and lead their graduates under the ideological guidance of their moral codes, these schools will survive and help many of their students along the way.

References

Al-Harthi, A. S. (2005). Distance higher education experiences of Arab Gulf students in the United States: A cultural perspective. *International Review of Research in Open and Distance Learning*, *6*(3).

Bell, Jr., D. A. (1995). Racial realism. In K. Crenshaw, N. Gotanda, G. Peller, and Thomas, Kendall (Eds.), *Critical Race Theory: The key writings that formed the movement* (302–312). New York: The New Press.

Boyd, D. (2012). White flight in networked publics?: How race and class shaped American teen engagement with MySpace and Facebook. In L. Nakamura and A. Chow-White (Eds.), *Race after the internet* (262–285). New York: Routledge.

Brookfield, S. D. (2005). *The power of critical theory.* San Francisco: Jossey-Bass.

De Vos, G. A. (2006). Introduction ethnic pluralism: Conflict and acommodation, the role of ethnicity in social history. In L. Romanucci-Ross, G. A. De Vos, and T. Tsuda (Eds.), *Ethnic identity: Problems and prospects for the twenty-first century* (4th ed., 1–36). New York: Altamira Press.

Du Bois, W. E. B., and Huggins, N. I. (1986). *Writings.* New York: Literary Classics of the United States.

Gudykunst, W. B. (1989). Culture and the development of interpersonal relationships. *Communication Yearbook, 12*, 315–354.

Gudykunst, W. B., Matsumoto, Y., Ting-Toomey, S., Nishida, T., Kim, K., and Heyman, S. (1996). The Influence of cultural individualism-collectivism, self construals, and individual values on communication styles across cultures. *Human Communication Research, 22*(4), 510–543.

Hall, E. T. (1976). *Beyond culture.* Anchor Press/Doubleday.

Hofstede, G., Hofstede, G. J., and Minkov, M. (2010). *Cultures and organizations: Software of the mind* (3rd ed.). McGraw Hill.

hooks, bell. (2003). *Rock my soul: Black people and self-esteem.* Washington Square.

Ibarra, R. A. (2000). *Studying Latinos in a "virtual" university: Reframing diversity and academic culture change* (Occasional Paper No. 68; Latino Studies Series).

Ladson-Billings, G., and Tate IV, W. F. (2006). Toward a Critical Race Theory of education. In A. D. Dixson and C. K. Rousseau (Eds.), *Critical Race Theory in education* (11–30). Routledge.

Nakamura, L., and Chow-White, A. (Eds.). (2012). *Race after the internet.* Routledge.

Nanton, C. R. (2005). *Through these gates: African diasporan women's decision to participate in adult education programs* [EdD diss.]. Columbia University.

Outlaw, L. T., Jr. (1996). *On race and philosophy.* Taylor and Francis.

Steele, C. M. (2009). A threat in the air: How stereotypes shape intellectual identity and performance. In E. Taylor, D. Gillborn, and G. Ladson-Billings (Eds.), *Foundations of Critical Race Theory in education* (163–189). Routledge.

Sweeting, A., and Westbrook, T. (2021). Stronger together: A faith inspired resistance to racism in higher education. *Journal of Graduate Education Research*, *2*, 9–13.

Toprak, E., and Kumtepe, E. G. (Eds.). (2018). *Supporting multiculturalism in open and distance learning spaces.* IGI Global.

Verschelden, C. (2017). *Bandwidth recovery: Helping students reclaim cognitive resources lost to poverty, racism, and social marginalization.* Sterling, VA: Stylus.

West, C. (2001). *Race matters.* Boston: Beacon.

Westbrook, T. (2014). Global contexts for learning: Exploring the relationship between low-context online learning and high-context learners. *Christian Higher Education*, *13*(4), 281–294.

Westbrook, T. (2017). *Spirituality, community, and race consciousness in adult higher education: Breaking the Cycle of Racialization.* New York: Routledge.

11

Flipped Classrooms: Reshaping the Tyndale Degree Completion Program for Engagement and Learning

Lawrence Hopperton

Distributed Learning and the Flipped Classroom

The flipped classroom lies on the spectrum of distributed learning. Distributed learning is a continuum with 19th and 20th century classroom models at one end, to completely online, multi-media and multi-modal presentations at the other end. Under the definition of Distributed Learning specified by Hopperton (2015), any course that uses any aspect of technology in its delivery is on the distributed learning continuum. This can be as simple as posting a syllabus online to the applications of virtual reality. But the flipped-classroom does not define a particular point on the spectrum; rather, it is a best use of resources, including technology, to maximize the learning experience of the students. Figure 1.1 illustrates this idea.

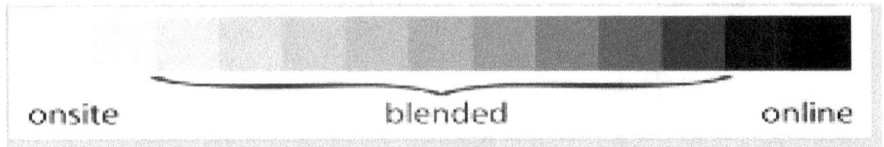

Figure 1.1 Degrees of flipped classrooms on the
distributed learning continuum.

The blending of technology and teaching in the flipped classroom provides flexibility for the professor, the student, and the program.

Flipped/Mixed-Mode/Blended Classrooms

There is no one definition of flipped classrooms. The broadest definition, drafted by the Sloan-C Foundation (Picciano, 2007) states,

- Courses integrate online with traditional face-to-face activities in a planned, pedagogically valuable manner, and

- A portion (institutionally defined) of face-to-face time is replaced by online activity.

The general agreement is that a flipped classroom provides pre-recorded audio/video presentations followed by in-class activity. Students view the content material before class so that the freed lecture time can be devoted to interaction including Q&A, discussions, exercises, or other learning activities. "Flipped classrooms" refers to any teaching model that replaces in-class lecture with pre-developed media elements with the goal to use freed-up time for elaboration, interactivity, and student-centered customization. It involves an

Integration of online and face-to-face instruction to promote engagement and improve outcomes.

These are broad definitions, and figure 1.1 illustrates the range of their variability. The flipped classroom involves an integration of online and face-to-face activities for their best purposes in order to promote engagement and improved student learning (D2L, 2014). It blends physical and online activities in order to create an optimal learning experience for the purpose of improving outcomes (Stein, 2014).

According to the systematic instructional design model (Dick and Carey, 2015), the pedagogical plan recommends that institutions and faculty consider the variables of learning for a five-week course, and incorporate each variable for its greatest effect. This challenges our traditional perceptions of post-secondary education, questioning the assumption of the preeminence of the classroom to what is the best use of resources for student learning. Is lecturing the best use of limited classroom time in a DCP course, or is it only a current necessary reality?

This is a question of the best applications of resources, given the requirements of credit course delivery. Since the flipped classroom is defined as a spectrum along a continuum, the question concerns what variables are involved in the placement of a learning instance along the spectrum. How can we maximize the impact of each variable in order to augment student learning? Table 1.1 presents a simplified form of the consideration of variables.

Time	Synchronous	Asynchronous
Place	F2F	Online
Pedagogy	Cooperative	Competitive
Technology	Text	Multi media
Format	Cohort	Self-paced
Courses	Home institution	Other
Participants	Local	Distant

Table 1.1 Broad variables in considering flipped classrooms

There are distinct advantages to incorporating the flipped classroom in the curriculum. Since these approaches are designed to leverage the use of online and face-to-face settings in ways that support knowledge, understanding, and transfer (Shea, 2007), they lend a more efficient use of class time which can become focused on elaboration rather than basic knowledge, as well as interactive learning activities such as discussion, group work, and application of knowledge. Instruction can either begin in the classroom and continue online, or begin online and continue in the classroom. If online discussion forums are included in the instructional design, these faculty-facilitated discussions provide equal access to the content and the professor at the convenience of the student (Thomson, 2015). In addition, the design can also include elements such as video conferencing, podcasting, reflective journaling, and other media.

Lecturing in the classroom is largely a passive, professor-focused activity. While there may be opportunities for some student questions, discussion is often limited by the time required to transfer knowledge. Active learning opportunities provide for increased engagement and interaction in a learner-centered environment, including connected-ness, collaboration, access, and convenience.

Advantages and Responsibilities for Students, Faculty, and Institutions

These are all positive features for the student, but they do come at a cost, particularly with shortened teaching periods. Students must take direct and personal responsibility for their own learning and be familiar with the materials presented through alternative media.

For faculty, since the design process considers the best use of each learning element, it provides a new flexibility for achieving optimal student outcomes (D2L, 2014) that are consistent with those expected of students in face-to-face or fully online courses. Teaching methods need to be adjusted and the computer-mediated elements of the course need to be created and produced before the launch of the class. These elements could include voice over PowerPoint lectures, video lectures, online forums, posted readings, internet links, or Zoom office hours. Faculty will require training, developmental and systemic support (Vignare, 2007) throughout this process. Fortunately, once the flip has been created, it can be reused next time the course is offered since core knowledge remains fairly stable over time, while elaboration and customization to the individual groups of students is more fluid.

As designers of the flipped classroom, we need to consider the best use of each alternative and to design our courses accordingly. As a faculty member, what can I do with this flexible alternative form in order to enhance the learning experience? What is the most efficient and effective use of each variable, given the institutional constraints and our focus on student-centered learning? Under the flipped classroom, a course is not about the delivery of content within a prescribed environment; rather, it is learning focused upon self-motivation and responsibility within the requirements of the institution. This requires intentional course design (Stein, 2014) and the scheduling and production of media elements within the required adherence to institutional standards specified through common learning outcomes for all instances of the same course.

In distributed learning applications at Tyndale, it is assumed that if two professors teach the same course with identical outcomes, there will be variations in the presentation. Distributed learning at Tyndale incorporates an 80/20 guideline: 80% of content is consistent across all sections and is sufficient for the successful achievement of the learning outcomes, and 20% of content is variable, dependent upon the faculty member.

Time for completing a course is an easy comparison to use when comparing face-to-face classes to compressed, flipped classrooms. The Carnegie unit provides a method for calculating student hours required for a course. In essence, each hour spent in class will require two hours of student work outside the class. Using this model, 3-credit face-to-face classes provide 3 hours per week of direct faculty instruction in addition to 6 hours per week of homework over a period of 15 weeks. When the federal definition of a clock hour (50 minutes) is factored into this equation, the time reduces to 2.5 hours per week of direct faculty instruction and 5 hours per week of homework over a period of 15 weeks. This is a commitment on the part of the students, then, of 37.5 hours of engagement with direct faculty instruction plus 75 hours of engagement with homework totaling 112.5 hours per 3-

credit course in order to achieve the learning outcomes. This is the time model that we should consider bringing to the compressed course format. Although we have shortened the duration of the course, the time requirement for success has really not changed.

Building and Implementing the Flipped Classroom

The flipped classroom is not a one-size-fits-all approach. It assumes that faculty will bring their individual approaches to the developmental process and application. As a result, the general model that says technology will be incorporated is flexible. For compressed classes delivered in limited time frames, it retains basic time commitments of students while providing faculty with the opportunity to contextualize learning for individuals and classes. For the Tyndale DCP program, it offers the ability to enhance academic credibility of alternative modes of learning while augmenting student learning.

References

Hopperton, L. (2015). Distributed Learning. *The Sage Encyclopedia of Online Learning*, Vol. 1. Ed. Steven Danvers. Washington: Sage Publishing.

Picciano, A. G. (2007). Introduction to blended learning: Research perspectives. In Anthony G. Picciano and Charles D. Dziuban (Eds.). *Blended learning: Research perspectives*. Newburyport: Sloan-C. pp 5-18.

Desire to Learn (D2L) Corporation (2014). *Blended learning: Where teaching meets technology.* White paper. Sydney, Australia.

Dick, W., Carey, L., and Carey, James O. (2014). *The systematic design of instruction*, 8th edition. London: Pearson Educational Publishing.

Shea, Peter (2007). Towards a conceptual framework for learning in blended environments. In Anthony G. Picciano and Charles D. Dziuban (Eds.). *Blended learning: Research perspectives.* Newburyport: Sloan-C. pp 19-36.

Thomson, R., Fichten, C., Budd, J., Havel, A. and Ascuncion, J. (2015). Blending universal design, e-learning, and information and communication technologies. In S.E. Burgstahler (Ed.), *Universal design in higher education: From principles to practice* (2nd ed.), 275-284. Boston: Harvard Educational Press.

Vignare, Karen (2007). Review of the literature on blended learning. In Anthony G. Picciano and Charles D. Dziuban (Eds.). *Blended learning: Research perspectives.* Newburyport: Sloan-C. pp 137-64.

Stein, Jared, and Graham, Charles R. (2014). *Essentials for blended learning: A standards based guide.* Taylor and Frances Group: Milton Park, UK.

12

Building an Online Course for the Catholic Distance Learning Network: Teaching Theology and Science in Cyberspace[1]

Sebastian Mahfood and Michael Hoonhout

In the summer of 2007, the Catholic Distance Learning Network (CDLN) offered a course on online teaching and learning to 11 faculty members from eight seminaries and theological institutions. The schools represented in the course (Kenrick-Glennon Seminary in St. Louis, MO; St. Paul School of Divinity in St. Paul, MN; Catholic Theological Union in Chicago, IL; the University of St. Thomas School of Theology at St. Mary's Seminary in Houston, TX; St. Mary Seminary in Cleveland, OH; Holy Apostles College and Seminary in Cromwell, CT; Seminary of the Immaculate Conception in Huntington, NY; and St. Meinrad School of Theology in St. Meinrad, IN) were preparing to offer their first courses to one another's students in the spring and fall of 2008.

---

[1] This chapter was first published in *Seminary Journal*, Vol. 13, No. 2, Fall 2007, 60-67. Reprinted with permission. See seminaryjournal.com.

The Premise on which this Online Course was Built

The courses developed for the spring of 2008 promoted the global vision initiative that drove the network, engaging the areas of evangelization/inculturation, ecumenism/unity, interfaith dialogue, and authentic human relationships. Topics included religious pluralism; the shaping of places for worship; liturgy and the art of ritual; the ethics of power and racial justice; the history, theology, and pastoral applications of the liturgical year; the psalms as Christian prayer; the theology of the priesthood of Jesus Christ in Hebrews; inter-religious dialogue; and the relationship between theology and science. It was hoped that the development and offering of courses like these would strengthen the efforts of seminaries to collaborate in sharing human and material resources with one another.

Developing the network as a means by which to bring resources together involved a commitment on the part of seminaries and theological institutes to open themselves to the possibility of a new teaching model—that of the entirely online classroom within the face-to-face, or residential, community. This model required that lecture content and the activities appropriate for interaction with the lecture be made accessible in cyberspace. It also required that faculty and students communicated with one another through discussion boards and chat rooms rather than physically come together at the same time within the same place.

The advantages of the former were explored by theological education in the first decade of this century as seminaries transitioned into hybrid courses where faculty began using course templates to house their content and provide means by which students might prepare for their face-to-face courses. This was the bridge, which strengthened the versatility of instructional design by combining lecture materials with complementary lab activities. The community of learners could also interact more dialogically with one another, which meant that in every learning experience everyone could be encouraged to engage more fully one another's ideas both immediately and over time after considered reflection. A residential online learning environment, then, could be a viable means by which to do theological studies.

To explore this idea of whether distance learning could work within a residential community, Kenrick-Glennon Seminary offered in the spring of 2005 an online course in Dante's Divine Comedy to its seminarians and extended the invitation to the archdiocesan priests in St. Louis. The opportunity drew 12 students, 10 of whom were residential, who went through one canto a day for 100 days. Members of the class were provided access every morning to a new webpage that explored some of the issues within each of the areas through which Dante traveled on his way to the celestial vision.

Interaction was through a blog posted on each of the webpages, and students were required to develop online their semester project over one aspect of Dante's journey. While much of the content dissemination could have been accomplished in a traditional classroom setting, the online experience enabled the course professor to embed at appropriate moments within the course 150 video clips from interviews with 20 theology teachers who had on-site teaching responsibilities, drawing the entire faculty into the interpretation of the world of Dante based on pagan mythology and medieval scholasticism. The success of this experience was also measurable in how it demonstrated the way in which interdisciplinary involvement could so easily be achieved in cyberspace.

At this point in the development of the educational technology initiatives of many Catholic seminaries, we knew that a growing number of faculty had begun to have a presence on the Web and were producing materials for dissemination to their students via cyberspace—in whatever form that took, email, discussion boards, podcasts, and standard Web pages. We also knew that with a little organization, a lot of this developing material could be packaged in the form of discrete learning modules that could be brought together to form the content for an entire online course. Beyond this, a great many of the classes that were still delivered in the traditional face-to-face manner had content that was already organized and, therefore, likely ready for modulation within a course template.

Merely posting our content online, though, was not enough to take advantage of the transformative environment that the World Wide Web provides. We had to find a way to make our content interactive and engaging, a way to satisfy the needs of a community of learners who gathered for dialogue around it. Once we did that, we were better able to realize the promise of cyberspace as a community-building tool capable of bringing together a myriad of cultures.

Given the opportunities that an online course brings to a single residential community, it was a small conceptual step to the realization that an online course also might have value for multiple residential communities. Colleges and universities already have done the fieldwork in the development for credit of not only online coursework but also of whole degree programs. People who live hundreds of miles from a given institution of learning (or who live only five minutes away) can complete classes and earn degrees online. The online learning experience is versatile in dealing with scheduling conflicts to which traditional courses, set in a certain time and at a certain place, are prone. Online teaching and learning, then, is already a viable means of credentialing, and it is already recognized by both regional and professional accrediting agencies. The challenge for us as educators in theological studies within communities not only of learning but also of formation, then, is no longer to make efforts to determine whether online learning works—we know it does—but to find ways to make it work for us. In pursuing this, we first need to be clear about what it is we want to accomplish, which is simply to use the new collaborative processes the Web makes possible to share our courses with one another and to explore the new vistas that will arise because of it.

The Catholic Distance Learning Network, which was designed to be a structure through which faculty in seminaries and theological institutes could offer their courses online, not only provided pedagogical training and instructional design support to faculty, but it also had a responsibility to navigate the participating institutions through the various challenges each faced coordinating the enrollment and administration of the students. These two concerns had the potential to overlap fairly often within the context of a network dedicated to Catholic institutions that varied in terms of their degree programs and students even though they all shared the primary purpose of forming men for the priesthood in the United States. Some institutions, for instance, enrolled into their courses only those seeking ordination while others open themselves to the laity pursuing theological degrees. The problem that this created was the need to apply a general assessment structure to a diverse student population while not losing the ethos of the sponsoring institution in the transaction.

The resolution was to rely on the basic nature of online courses, which, because they seek to model and build collaborative communities of learning, are necessarily activity-based. Each activity within a given course was able to demonstrate a relationship with one or more of the learning outcomes just as each of the learning outcomes on a given syllabus was able to demonstrate a relationship with one or more of the program outcomes of the institution from which the course was being offered. This tied each of the activities to the mission statement to ensure that each course continued to promote the integrity of the institution that was sponsoring it, even if it was heavily dominated by students originating elsewhere.

In working through avoidable problems like these, the network fostered a culture of planning that sustained the mission of strengthening the relationship among its member institutions. Aside from establishing an administrative structure, the network had a mission to promote exemplary teaching practices in the professors it certified in distance learning. It did this by offering an eight-week online summer course in online teaching and learning and providing each of the participating faculty with an on-site instructional designer who shepherded him or her through the technical training that is necessarily advanced alongside the pedagogical training. The goal was to enable each of the participating faculty to have confidence in the prospect of offering a course online by providing that person with at least the minimum skill sets in the technical aspects of online course development.

One example of this can be found in the development of a course titled "Theology and Science," which was designed by a dogmatic theologian from the Seminary of the Immaculate Conception in Huntington, NY. The goal of the course is to provide an understanding of how to integrate the findings of modern science with the Christian teaching on creation to produce a contemporary theological cosmology—that is, a view of the natural world as God's work of glory that incorporates even as it transcends the findings of science. It also gives students opportunities to develop the pastoral skills needed to communicate this theonomous vision of reality to others and to answer the reductions of scientific materialism and creation science. It was being offered online in part because of the wealth of pertinent materials available on the Web: governmental and education sites dedicated to the teaching and history of science, numerous cultural examples in cyberspace of a conflicting relationship or inadequate integration between science and theology, and the power of graphic media to convey the startling beauty and intricate order found in God's manifold creation.

The online format also allows what is essentially an elective course to draw a larger, more diverse and more interested group of students than would normally be found among the seminarian and lay students at the home institution. The professor had taught the subject before in a traditional classroom setting, and thus had a course structure, notes, and resources materials to draw upon. What the professor did in preparation for the teaching experience was to modulate his lecture materials and embed various activities within each module, establishing a systematic process that is easily transferable to other online courses he might create for the network.

Converting the Face-to-Face Course to an Online Course

Converting the face-to-face syllabus to an online syllabus is more than merely reparsing the lecture materials and integrating activities; it requires rethinking the idea of a learning community that is gathering not physically but cognitively around a particular set of materials based on a specific topic of interest. Students in online courses are present to one another entirely and only through their active participation in the various discussion forums (either synchronous or asynchronous) created by the professor. They are present, that is, only through the texts they offer the community and only in the interaction with texts offered by others within the community. For that reason, the activities in each week of the course have to provide a context for students to engage one another and the professor. Their active engagement of the materials takes many forms, such as posting to discussion threads, individual or collaborative project-development, short essay writing, journaling on blogs and the like, but is always community oriented.

These collaborative activities in turn become the basis for their evaluation. In reflecting the ethos of a community of learners, then, the syllabus for an online course has to weigh participation more heavily than would the syllabus for a face-to-face course, both explicitly in the stated objectives and expectations of the course and implicitly in the way interactive assignments are designed to demonstrate student learning to all engaged in the online course, in contrast to the traditional feedback of written papers and exams viewed only by the professor in a face-to-face course.

For an online course, then, any given week should have a structure that facilitates this kind of community interaction. The overall structure for each week can follow a set pattern (since this facilitates student engagement with the online learning process) even as particular components in that structure vary from week to week (since this helps sustain that engagement). Like most online courses, the general format to the structure of "Theology and Science" is threefold: initial orientation, individual learning of material, interactive and collaborative assignments that demonstrate and reinforce that learning. The first part, the orientation that initiates each week, consists of an opening prayer, introduction of the week's topic, and overview of the week's assignments. Next, the learning of the material by each student occurs through the watching of a video lecture by the professor and the reading of the assigned course texts. Finally, the students are asked to complete varying online assignments designed to give him or her the opportunity to reiterate, share and apply what they have learned with others in the course. Let us look at these specific elements more closely.

Although, as an online course, "Theology and Science" is offered outside of a seminary's communal prayer life, as a theological course with pastoral implications it does not wish to lose on account of the cyber setting the important role of prayer for theology. Since it intends to foster a theological vision of creation rooted in the praise of God, every week's module begins with an appropriate prayer, such as a creation hymn from the Book of Psalms or the Canticle of Creation by St. Francis of Assisi. Despite the inability to gather the community in real time and a common place, each week begins with a short video of the professor's reading aloud the psalm or prayer. The students are required to follow along with the scriptural passage or prayer text before them and pray along with the professor, to inculcate the praise of God and gratitude for creation that is the basis for a theological engagement of nature. Although the online members will engage in this exercise asynchronously, their sincere engagement will still allow them to pray together as one in Christ, even if not at the same time or place.

The next element in the structure is a short orientation to the week. The orientation for week two, for instance, reads as follows:

This week's primary topic is the relation between science and theology. What you need to learn are the different models that those who have done some reflection on this topic have proposed. There exist different models for the relationship between these two disciplines because in our world today there are some who see science and theology in competition and conflict, others who think that it would be best if the two were understood as distinct with little overlap, and others who believe that a deep integration of the two is possible. To give these models names, the first is a model of Confrontation, the second is Separation, and the third is Correlation. These models will prove very helpful throughout the course in giving a framework for understanding the many historical moments and particular questions where science and theology both have something to say about the created world. Knowing them also can help you to be ambassadors in your pastoral ministries to personally model a coherent and helpful integration of these two disciplines and perspectives to those fearful of either science or religion.

The written orientation provides the context for the 20-minute audio lecture that will follow. This lecture, in order to reveal itself fully to the listener, cannot simply be 20 straight minutes of unbroken audio—it has to bear within itself the possibility of being stopped, explored, and restarted—just like what would happen to some degree in a face-to-face class when a student raises his or her hand to interrupt the lecture and ask a clarifying question. For that reason, the lecture, which is synched to a PowerPoint slideshow, has stops embedded on many slides with links that take the viewer to a public questions blog page or a clarifying activity that offers the viewer some engagement with the material before he or she can continue to the next point. To be inclusive of students who have physical hearing impairments or technological limitations on their computers that preclude audio—or even of students who prefer to print things out for easy reference later—each lecture is also available in text form. To accommodate those who like to take the lecture on the road with their iPods, the lectures are also available in .mp3. Each lecture is followed by a selection of readings that support the lecture and develop the topic further.

Just as in a real-world classroom the readings and lecture would be followed by discussion and demonstration exercises (e.g., papers and exams) that make the connection between what has been learned and the student's experience, so too in this online learning module the readings are followed by various assignments that foster appropriation and overcome the possible isolation of online learning by being highly collaborative. Online, asynchronous discussion takes place in dedicated forums, with the professor seeding the conversation with initial questions based on the readings, and the students themselves developing and sustaining the dialogue by offering their own interpretations and responding to the postings of others.

The discussion of the material is complemented with various online activities, again designed for collaborative engagement and providing an opportunity for the student to demonstrate understanding, which in turn serves as a basis for the professor's assessment of the students' work. In the case of the second week of "Theology and Science," the reading material on the different models for the relationship between theology and science is reinforced by an Internet scavenger hunt:

> Students will find examples from the Web exemplifying each of the different models (could be text, audio, video) and post these in the discussion forum for others to view with their own arguments as to why each fits that model (reasons taken from assigned reading and lecture). If students find that they disagree with someone's classification of a posting, they should respond with their reasons as to why another model is a better fit.

This activity invests the student in the determinative reasons for each model and provides them with a basis for internalizing the point of the lecture. Yet the work of each student is viewed and evaluated by all the others, not just the professor. The communal posting gives other students the opportunity to work and learn together, even as it gives the professor a concrete basis for assessing the quality of each student's learning. These discussion forums and related activities are dedicated to the understanding and application of the ideas and concepts in the course, treating the analytical aspects of the history, relation, and methodologies of theology and science. Yet when the assigned readings concern the more aesthetic or theological appreciation of nature as God's creation, which is a related but different goal of the course, the students are expected to respond differently, in a manner that corresponds to this objective. Instead of posting in discussion forums, the students will journal in their own personal blogs set up for the course, as well as read and respond to the blogs of others. These personal blogs—consisting not just of personal reflections but also of relevant links and media that show the beauty and design of God's creation—will also serve as a semester-long project, with a vote at the end for best in quality. An example of this kind of activity, again from the second week of the course, reads as follows:

> After completion of the readings, blog in your personal journal a response to one of the following reflection questions:
>
> a. What are the instances in your life when you felt your religious faith or viewpoint threatened by science?
> b. What pastoral situations have you experienced in which the tendency to separate science and theology was a wise approach to take?
> c. What are the characteristics of someone in your personal life who exemplifies for you an integrated understanding of science and theology?

The idea behind asking the students to choose one of three questions is a pedagogical strategy called choice-making. Choice-making provides students with a sense of control over the prompt they choose and creates areas of fresh discussion within the two areas they did not choose. Students are expected to review one another's blogs and may find themes in other perspectives or on other prompts that inspire reflection and comment.

An important consideration for designing weekly activities within a course involves the time commitment expected of the students. Although the professor can design the activities first and then add up the time needed to complete all the assignments for a particular week, it is better to start from a standard formula to determine the expected time commitment and fit the online activities within that time frame. This is a matter of taking the time standards expected for a face-to-face course, based on course credits, and adjusting them for the online setting. The USDE has done this for us in the form of the Carnegie unit (a way to define the credit hour, which may be cross-referenced with the clock hour of 50 minutes). While face-to-face courses separate the student's time commitment between the hours spent together in class and the individual hours dedicated to reading, studying, and writing, online courses group these weekly hours together and expect the student to dedicate the same amount of total hours to the course, giving the student both the flexibility and responsibility to fill those hours throughout the whole week. Since each face-to-face class meets for approximately one clock hour each week per credit hour, and then expects another two clock hours for individual learning outside of class, one can expect from the student an average of 2.5 hours per credit each week. Thus a 3-credit course requires a weekly time commitment of 7.5 hours, and a 2-credit course about 5 hours.

In applying the same time expectation for each week of an online course, one needs to calculate how long each activity should take and add up the hours. Reading assignments take the same amount of time, approximately one hour for every 25 pages of text. A 20-minute audio lecture with embedded links to various Web sites or to supporting materials in the form of text, audio, or video, will take longer than the 20 minute length of the presentation because of the time needed to follow up on those embedded discussions—about an hour in total.

Discussion board activity requires ample time for reading and responding. Students typically will need 30 minutes to read discussion threads and take up to 20 to 30 minutes to develop and post their own comments. Writing thoughtful reflections for one's own blog can take 40 minutes, with more time need for reading the blogs of others. Time needs to be built in, too, for the collaborative projects students are expected to accomplish over the course of several weeks. In ways like this, one can calculate how long one is asking the student to interact with the course, although it can at best be only an estimate given that some students will require more time to read and write than others (as happens in face-to-face courses). To prevent slow Internet connections from significantly lengthening the time a student needs to engage the course material and complete activities, the minimum technological requirements for the course are posted prior to course registration, with a medium- to high-speed connection being a technological prerequisite for admission.

As far as accountability exercises, it is best to have only one per credit hour. A 2-credit face-to-face class might have a paper and an exam, and a 3-credit face-to- face class might have a paper, a project, and an exam. In the world of online teaching, exams are rarely very helpful since they always have to be considered open-book, for the goal is not to test memory but facility with the materials, and exams cannot be done collaboratively. Three-credit online courses may go the route of participation/interaction/collaboration (say, a formal discussion board and a reflective blog), a project (done in pieces throughout the semester culminating in a 3-page paper and a 15-minute presentation), and an activity-set (say, a handful of really short assignments spread out over the duration of the course). Whatever method is used, the time it would take an average person to engage each week ought to be tabulated so that no week gets over-loaded, a good reason for breaking larger projects into smaller ones.

Since "Theology and Science" is a 3-credit course, assessment of students is based upon three sets of activities: the weekly assignments and two extended projects, one individual and one group. Participation is evaluated weekly in terms of the quantity and quality of the student's contributions to the discussion forums. The accomplishment of individual week activities, such as the Internet scavenger hunt, are to be judged in terms of how well the student has demonstrated his or her grasp of the principles or issues in lecture and reading materials. The individual project is the personal blog or journal, evaluated by the class at the end of the semester in terms of quality of construction and impact upon others. The group project is the construction of a historical timeline of the relation between theology and science, with groups of three students working together on a different period to show both the contributions of historical figures and the paradigm shifts in theological and scientific worldviews.

Conclusion

All the work that goes into the development of an online course is meaningful for the development of face-to-face courses because pedagogical strategies will transfer into hybrid classroom environments. It is for this reason that the Catholic Distance Learning Network considered its efforts as broader than its stated mission to train faculty within the Catholic seminaries to teach online for the purpose of institutional collaboration in the offering of online courses.

The way it worked is that when a professor made the choice to offer his or her course through the network, he or she first worked with the academic dean to schedule it as part his or her regular teaching load for electives. It was first offered to the students at the host institution. If those students filled all 15 slots, the course would be closed to other participating schools. If the course did not fill all 15 of its virtual seats, the number of remaining seats were given away free of charge to students in participating schools on a first-come-first-served registration basis. Each host institution developed its own policies for administration of their online course offerings beyond these guidelines.

As we approached the first round of course offerings in the spring of 2008, we expected that our experiment, which began with 23 academic deans and rectors attending the National Catholic Education Association's pre-convocation workshop in the fall of 2006, would continue to prove to be a valuable means for collaboration among Catholic seminaries in ways we could not then express. We were not disappointed.

The Catholic Distance Learning Network ended its work among

the seminaries in 2012 but continues to this day in a new form – that of over 200 courses offered by the faculty of two dozen seminaries who teach as adjuncts within the online programs at Holy Apostles College and Seminary in Cromwell, CT.

Contributor Biographies

Dave Bland, Ph.D., is professor of preaching at Harding School of Theology, where he has taught for twenty-eight years. He also co-directs the Doctor of Ministry program. He continues to teach on-line education primarily through HSTLIVE. He holds the Doctor of Ministry degree from Western Seminary in Portland, Oregon and the Ph.D. from University of Washington in Seattle.

Matthew Boutilier, Ph.D., is the Associate Dean of Online Education at Trinity International University, an Adjunct Professor in their Biblical and Religious Studies department, and Chair of the Online Committee. He has been involved in online education professionally since 2011 in a teaching capacity as well as an instructional designer. In addition to his teaching responsibilities at TIU, he also teaches at Clarks Summit University (Bible and Theology Department) and the University of Wisconsin-Whitewater (Instructional Design and Learning Technology). Boutilier has earned his M.Div. with a concentration in Systematic Theology from Baptist Bible Seminary. He also earned his M.S.Ed in Curriculum and Instruction (concentration in Learning Design and Technology) from Purdue University. He completed his Ph.D. in Educational Studies at Trinity Evangelical Divinity School.

Victoria Dunnam, Ph.D., currently is an Educational Technology Consultant for Union Theology Seminary, a Moodle Administrator, a Quality Reviewer/ Learning Architect for iDesign and is an Instructional Designer and Content Developer for online courses for universities, as well as an adjunct online instructor. She owns and operates Dunnam Consulting. She completed her doctorate from Grand Canyon University with Ph.D. in Psychology with Emphasis on Integrated Technology and Learning, She holds a Master's Degree in Educational Technology from University of Texas in Brownsville and a BBA Computer Science degree from Hardin Simmons University. She is a member of the executive committee for Faith-Based Online Directors (FOLD) organization. Her interests and passion is online learning and creating quality online course design that impacts student's online learning experience.

Deborah Hayes, Ed.D., who passed away in 2018, was an Associate Professor of Education at Carson-Newman University. Dr. Hayes was engaged in all aspects of the university academic community and was affiliated with multiple scholarly and professional entities. Her expertise included online and distance learning, the impact of assessment on curriculum, and innovative online instruction. The Dr. Deborah Hayes Distinguished Dissertation Award, created in her memory, is awarded annually to the Carson Newman doctoral graduate whose dissertation most exemplifies Dr. Hayes' values of excellence and exemplary research skills. Dr. Hayes received her Ed.D. in Educational Administration and Supervision from the University of Tennessee.

Rebecca Hoey, Ed.D., is Northwestern's dean for the Graduate School and Adult Learning. She oversees development of the college's graduate degrees and other programs for adult learners. These include graduate pro-grams in education, physician assistant studies, athletic training, graduate certificates and degree-completion programs in nursing (RN-BSN) and early childhood education as well as continuing education opportunities. While a research committee member for the International Association for K-12 Online Learning, she helped write a survey of policy and practices around the world. Dr. Hoey is co-editor of *NET: An e-Journal of Faith-Based Distance Learning*, and she has published in the *Online Journal of Distance Learning Administration*. Northwestern's 2020 recipient of the Faculty Inspirational Service Award, she has experience teaching online courses and developing and designing online curriculum. Prior to entering higher education, she taught business in high schools in Colorado and Minnesota.

Michael Hoonhout, Ph.D., is a professor of dogmatic theology at St. Joseph's Seminary in Yonkers, NY since 2013; previously he taught at the Seminary of the Immaculate Conception in Huntington on Long Island, NY. He obtained his doctorate in systematic theology from Boston College, and in his research and presentations strives to incorporate the cosmology of modern science within the theology of creation and divine providence of St. Thomas Aquinas. He has taught courses online, via hybrid models, and is committed to offering both in his Seminary's new online degree program. He is currently in formation to become a permanent deacon in the Catholic Church.

Lawrence Hopperton, Ph.D., (retired) is the founding Director of the Center for Distributed Learning at Tyndale University in Canada. He has been involved in online education since the early 1980's, initially as editor for Mathematics, Engineering, and Computer Science. Following the completion of a Masters of Education in educational change and a doctorate focused on online learning and instructional design for post-secondary and adult students from the University of Toronto, he served as Director of Research for the Canadian TeleLearning National Centres of Excellence and senior designer for the Canadian Centres of Excellence for Refugee and Immigrant studies. He currently serves as a member of the executive committee for the Faith-based Online Learning Directors and is a member of the Association for Christian Distance Education. He has published extensively on instructional design, institutional structures for distributed learning, and disability accessibility in online learning.

Mary Lowe, Ed.D., is the Online Associate Dean at the John W. Rawlings School of Divinity at Liberty University. She previously served as the Associate Dean of the Virtual Campus at Erskine Seminary and has been working in the field of online Christian education for more than 25 years. Mary is the Executive Director of ACCESS, the Association for Christian Distance Education. One of the areas of particular interest is the issue of spiritual formation in an online environment and she continues to write and research in this field. Mary is a co-editor of the 2012 book, "Best Practices for Online Education: A Guide for Christian Higher Education." Both Mary and her husband Steve co-directed the National Consultation on Spiritual Formation in Theological Distance Education funded by the Wabash Center for Teaching and Learning in Theology and Religion. Their latest book is *Ecologies of Faith in a Digital Age: Spiritual Growth Through Online Education*. She holds the doctorate in Instructional Technology and Distance Education.

Sebastian Mahfood, OP, Ph.D., has served full-time since 2012 on the faculty of Holy Apostles in Cromwell, CT, as Professor of Interdisciplinary Studies and Vice-President, after eleven years on the faculty of Kenrick-Glennon Seminary in St. Louis, MO. He has been a Lay Dominican of the Queen of the Holy Rosary Chapter in the Province of St. Albert the Great since 2008. His work in the areas of lay and priestly formation led him to found a Catholic publishing house called En Route Books and Media, which has produced a hundred and twenty titles since 2014, and an online Catholic radio station called WCAT Radio, which currently hosts about five dozen shows per week. Dr. Mahfood holds a doctorate in postcolonial literature and theory from Saint Louis University along with several master's degrees in the fields of comparative literature, philosophy, theology, and educational technology.

Fawn E. McCracken, Ed.D., is the Associate Vice President of Adult, Online, and Graduate Studies and Dean of the School of Online Studies and Graduate School at Crown College in Minnesota. She has been involved in curriculum design for online courses, online teaching, and administration of online degree programs since 2009. She has published and presented on distance education administration, online curriculum development, sense of community in online classrooms, and theory and practice in online degree programs. McCracken has earned her M.S. in Counseling Psychology from Palm Beach Atlantic University. She completed her Doctorate of Education with a concentration in online learning at Regent University.

Jordan Davis McDonald serves as the Children's Minister at Hunter Hills Church of Christ in Prattville, Alabama. She graduated from Harding University in 2017 with an undergraduate degree in Bible and Missions.

Morgan McGaughy works in community development at the Binghampton Development Corporation in Memphis, TN. She graduated from Harding University in 2017 with an undergraduate degree in Bible and Missions.

Sunday Akin Olukoju, Ph.D., earned his first master's degree in International Law and Diplomacy from the University of Lagos, his second master's degree in Educational Studies from Providence Theological Seminary, and he earned his PhD in Public Policy and Administration from Walden University. He has been serving in Immanuel Fellowship Church in Winnipeg Canada with his wife as lead pastors for over two decades, and he served as Providence Theological Seminary's Director of Distance Education. In addition to his role as an academic expert at Athabasca University, he continues to serve on the board of a few non-profit and community organizations in Canada.

Julia Price, Ed.D., is an Associate Professor of Education at Carson Newman University. Dr. Price is the Director of the Ed.D. and Ed.S. Advanced Programs and teaches Educational Leadership Graduate courses. She has designed and implemented multiple doctoral level online courses and has been active in online instruction since 2000. Her interests in this area include professor presence, course design, and productive course communication. Dr. Price is the recipient of the Carson Newman Advisor of the Year and the Carson Newman Research Award. She spent many years as a public school teacher and administrator and was a past Tennessee Principal of the Year. She completed her Ed.D. in Educational Leadership and Policy Design at East Tennessee State University.

Kelly Price, Ph.D., is an Associate Professor of Marketing at East Tennessee State University. Currently, she serves as coordinator for the online M.S. Digital Marketing and teaches several courses in the program. Dr. Price is a three-time recipient of the ETSU College of Business and Technology Excellence in Teaching Award and the Outstanding Teaching Award Emeritus Award. She has been involved in distance learning since 2005 and has published and presented within the areas of online education, consumer behavior, and women's golf. Kelly is also a current contributor to womensgolf.com. She completed her Ph.D. of Human Ecology at the University of Tennessee, Knoxville.

Timothy Paul Westbrook, Ph.D., is an associate professor of Bible and Ministry at Harding University and directs the Center for Distance Education in Bible and Ministry. He has been involved in distance education professionally since 2005 and has both published and presented on best practices and learning theory as they pertain to online course design. He sponsors the Black Student Association and is a member of the Critical Race Studies in Education Association. He serves as an executive officer for Faith-based Online Learning Directors (FOLD) and is a member of ACCESS and Society for Professors of Christian Education. Westbrook has earned his M.A. in doctrine and his M.Div. with a concentration in Old Testament from Harding School of Theology. He completed his Ph.D. in Educational Studies at Trinity Evangelical Divinity School.

www.ingramcontent.com/pod-product-compliance
Lightning Source LLC
Chambersburg PA
CBHW062202270326
41930CB00009B/1622